Christopher Hill, formerly Master of Balliol College, Oxford, then Professor of History at the Open University, has now retired. His many books include *God's Englishman* (1970), *The World Turned Upside Down* (1972), and *Change and Continuity in Seventeenth-Century England* (1975).

Some Intellectual Consequences
of the English Revolution

CHRISTOPHER HILL

A PHOENIX GIANT PAPERBACK

First published in Great Britain by George Weidenfeld and Nicolson in 1980
This paperback edition published in 1997 by Phoenix, a division of Orion Books Ltd,
Orion House, 5 Upper St Martin's Lane, London WC2H 9EA

A CIP catalogue record for this book is available from the
British Library.

ISBN: 0 75380 252 X

Printed and bound in Great Britain by
Butler & Tanner Ltd, Frome and London

The Merle Curti Lectures

To honour the distinguished historian Merle Curti, lectures in social and intellectual history were inaugurated in 1976 under the sponsorship of the University of Wisconsin Foundation and the Department of History of the University of Wisconsin-Madison.

I

THE RESTORATION in 1660 of a Parliament elected on the traditional franchise, of the House of Lords, monarchy, and the episcopal Church of England, brought the English Revolution to a close. The restoration reasserted the authority of the "natural rulers" of the country, the gentry and merchant oligarchies, both against any recrudescence of monarchical absolutism with episcopal support, such as had threatened under Charles I's personal government in the sixteen-thirties, and against a radical republic based on a democratic army, such as had emerged in the sixteen-forties and fifties. The restoration was thus two-faced. It wrote finis to the English Revolution; but it also confirmed many of the achievements of that most important event in English history.

These lectures were delivered in the bicentennial year of the American Revolution, and it seemed natural to reflect on parallels between the English and American Revolutions. Each was in due course followed by a period of world domination, which in England came to an end some 250 years after the Revolution. History looks different when we know the end of the story—in so far as any story ever really ends. So long as England was top nation, ruling the world, the seventeenth-century Revolution (in its widest sense, extending from 1640 to 1689) was seen as leading naturally and necessarily to the sovereignty of Parliament, the establishment of the Bank of England, to an aggressive commercial foreign policy, to the new intellectual syntheses of John Locke and Isaac Newton.

The Industrial Revolution and the supremacy of the British Empire followed inevitably.

But now the party is over. Even English historians no longer see the English constitution as the working out of a divine providence, God revealing representative government first to his Englishmen, then to his Americans. Sixteen eighty-eight no longer seems the decisive point on a continuing upward curve. The British Empire no longer exists; Britannia no longer rules the waves; we can no longer assume that Parliamentary government on the English model is necessarily applicable to or acceptable by emergent nations; industry and the pound have collapsed together. For all these and many other reasons the rival heritage of the sixteen-forties and fifties, and especially the policies defeated then, have come to seem to many historians at least as significant as the consensus of 1688.

I once thought of writing a book to be called *What Went Wrong?* in which I would trace the roots of Great Britain's decline (and transitory greatness) to the outcome of the seventeenth-century revolution, to the defeat of the more radical and democratic alternative strategies which were then put forward. There would have been something in it. But like most good ideas, it was over-simplified. Perhaps it is inevitable that small nations with limited economic resources should not be able to dominate the world political scene for very long: Venice, Spain, the Netherlands, France, Germany, Japan all tried and failed. The future may lie with super-powers—super in geographical extent, population, natural resources like the U.S.A., the U.S.S.R., China, Africa if it unites. But it may not: historians are bad prophets.

Anyway, in these lectures my intention was not to dwell on the familiar parts of the heritage of the English Revolution, which were stressed when Britain was still a world power and the U.S.A. seemed a promising heir apparent. They will be mentioned, inevitably; but my main stress will not be on Parliamentary sovereignty, on the rule of law, on how Locke led to the Enlightenment, or on the English genius for compromise. I shall emphasize rather more some of the flaws in the undoubted achievements of the seventeenth-century revolution, and shall look at the defeated alternatives, the might-have-beens. This is a less obvious approach than the traditional one, but it is perhaps more interesting with the hindsight which we now possess. It fits the sombre mood of post-imperial Britain, which badly needs historical explanations of how it got into its present plight; and the approach may not be totally irrelevant to the soul-searching going on in post-Vietnam, post-Watergate, racially conscious America.

My title recalls some earlier lectures which I published in 1965 as *Intellectual Origins of the English Revolution,* this title itself referring to Daniel Mornet's *Les Origines intellectuelles de la Révolution française.* In these lectures I dealt with Sir Francis Bacon and science, Sir Walter Ralegh and history and political theory, Sir Edward Coke and law. I now think it was perhaps a mistake to put so much emphasis on individuals, rather than on the trends of thought which they represent. But if I were to take individuals to represent the intellectual consequences of the English Revolution, Locke and Newton would select themselves: who would be the third? I think it would have to be John Milton—Milton perhaps as interpreted by Addison, Milton the great orthodox Puritan poet rather than the real Milton, republican and radical heretic. It is worth noting *en passant* that these three greatest figures in the intellectual history of the period all concealed secret heresies—anti-Trinitarianism, mortalism, millenarianism. The fact that they held such views, which could not be fully published even after 1688, tells us something important about post-restoration England. The establishment of the sort of society Milton had envisaged in *Areopagitica* was *not* one of the consequences of the English Revolution.

5

But the more I thought about the subject, the more doubtful I became about trying to isolate intellectual consequences of the Revolution, as I think it was possible to isolate intellectual causes. Before 1640 new ideas were challenging the existing society and its institutions. After the Revolution it is less easy to separate ideas from the society which the Revolution produced. So I hope I shall be forgiven if from time to time I seem to be broadening my subject by omitting the word "intellectual."

II

LET US START from the events of 1640–60, the main outlines of which I shall assume are familiar. Two problems worry me about traditional interpretations of the English Revolution. First, how this extraordinary event ever came about—not just the civil war of 1642–46, the execution of Charles I in 1649 and the republic of 1649–60, but the whole fantastic outburst of radical ideas and actions, spreading into all spheres of life and thought. Members of the ruling class were forced into positions which they never contemplated before the Revolution started—to regicide and the proclamation of a republic, to the abolition of the House of Lords, to land confiscations, to the abolition of episcopacy and acceptance of religious toleration, lay preaching, including preaching by women, several years of virtually complete freedom of the press, of organization and mobility for the lower classes. In these years the most unheard-of speculations were put forward, verbally and in print— demands for social and political equality, for a wide extension of the franchise, for abolition of a state church, for far-reaching social and legal reforms, for communism. All traditional institutions were called in question, including the Bible, private property, marriage and the family, male superiority. Where did all these fermenting ideas come from, many of them apparently without precedent in English history? Whence this tremendous intellectual and moral energy, greeted with such admiration by Milton in *Areopagitica*? That is not my theme in these lectures: I have tried to investigate it elsewhere[1] and to suggest

1. In *The World Turned Upside Down* (London: Penguin, 1975).

that perhaps the absolute novelty of the ideas may be an optical illusion resulting from the pre-1640 censorship; that more may have been going on below the surface of pre-revolutionary England than the books usually allow. I do not wish to argue this now: merely to insist on the existence of this background of revolutionary thought and activity in the middle decades of the century.

The second problem follows from the first. Where did it all go to? What happened to the radical revolutionary ideas, and the radical revolutionary thinkers, in the later seventeenth century? Was it all just an ephemeral frenzy, the product of loud-mouthed minorities? Did it all just run away into the sand? Even if this is the case, the mechanics by which this came about remain interesting. Emigration? Successful repression? If the latter, it was as effective as the Inquisition suppressing protestantism in Spain. How was it done? By taming the sects, who tamed their members? Was it George Fox in the seventeenth century rather than (as has been suggested) John Wesley in the eighteenth century who led the lower classes away from radical revolution in England? These are some of the questions that arise from these lectures.

A first answer will I am sure have occurred to many of my readers—that I have posed a pseudo-problem, that the radicals were always a tiny minority and their ideas influential only within a very limited sphere; that they appeared significant for a very short time, and only because a series of accidents put arms into their hands when acute divisions within the traditional ruling class had led to political breakdown and a collapse of authority; that nevertheless the power of the "natural rulers" of town and country, the gentry and merchants, was never seriously shaken, and after the restoration of 1660 simply re-asserted itself. This is the thesis contained in the lawyers' description of the Revolution as "the Interregnum": an eccentric interlude between two phases of normality, full of sound and fury, signifying nothing. As Professor Trevor-Roper suggested, there were no problems in 1641 which could not have been solved by sensible men sitting round a table.

Now this contains some truth, but not I think the whole truth. And it raises a host of other questions. No doubt the radicals were a minority; but so after all were the French and Russian revolutionaries at the beginning of their revolutions, yet their influence was or appears more lasting. And so too were the "natural rulers" a minority of the English population. Modern historians estimate the gentry in the sixteenth and seventeenth centuries at from 1 to 2 percent of the population. In Gregory King's tables of the sixteen-nineties, accepted respectfully by demographers, if we add together peers, bishops, baronets, knights, esquires, gentlemen, greater and lesser office-holders, merchants and traders by sea and land, lawyers —all those with incomes of more than £100 a year—they amount to only just over 3 percent of the population; and in some objective sense the ideas of the Levellers—say—would have come closer to representing the real interests of the majority of the population than the régime and the ideas which in fact prevailed in England for the century and three-quarters after 1688, under the rule of the Whig oligarchy. Perhaps the radicals simply did not have long enough to propagate their democratic ideas, so revolutionary in their novelty, among the 50 percent of the population which King classed as labourers, servants, cottagers and paupers, vagrants, seamen, and soldiers, those with incomes below £30 per annum; or among the 30 percent of lesser freeholders, farmers, shop-keepers and craftsmen with incomes of £40–50 a year. To break the centuries-old crust of custom would have needed longer than the three years in which the Levellers enjoyed liberty of propaganda and organization before being suppressed in 1649, more than the two decades in which the press was relatively free. This perhaps was part of what went wrong.

These are large issues, to which it is difficult to find direct answers. In these lectures I shall proceed by indirection, in the hope of arriving at some answers by implication. But I want to start by removing the idea that the potential influence of the radicals, their potential danger to the ruling class, is just a think-up of historians. The best way to do this, it seems to me, is to begin by having a look at the restoration, trying to strip it of the accumulated legends in which we are all brought up. For of course if the interregnum was just an unnatural interlude, then all Englishmen were pleased to welcome Charles II back in 1660; and the legend points to the dancing and singing in the streets, the burning of rumps, etc., as though they established the point. Even so eminent a scholar as Godfrey Davies tells us that the restoration "happened because the vast majority of Englishmen wanted it to happen." This begs every known question. How does he know? How does one measure a majority in 1660? Which Englishmen? Why did they want it to happen? Why was not only Charles II restored but also the House of Lords and the bishops? Did "the vast majority" want that too? How and why did the propertied class, so divided in 1641–46, and even more divided in the years after 1649, come to reunite so easily? To whose interest was it to assume that "the vast majority" wanted what they got?

There is plenty of contemporary evidence to throw doubt on the universality and spontaneity of rejoicing at Charles II's return. The royalist and Anglican Thomas Fuller wrote of the bonfires: "I believe the faggots themselves knew as much as some who laid them on for what purposes those fires were made." Ten years earlier Oliver Cromwell had said to Major-General Lambert, of a similarly enthusiastic crowd: "These very persons would shout just as much if you and I were going to be hanged." The royalist Sir John Reresby noted of Charles II's return that "a considerable number could have wished it otherwise" (and he listed many categories of these); but they "durst not oppose the current by seeming otherwise." William Prynne was one of these, who said "If Charles Stuart is to come in," it would be "better for those that waged war against his father that he should come in by their votes." Samuel Pepys was another. He signed a loyal address from the navy, so that "if it should come in print my name may be at it." For Pepys too, like so many others, had a past to live down. In 1649 he had expressed joyful approval of the execution of Charles I. Fortunately for him, the address was published.

In the year of the restoration John Corbet asked: "What was it that brought home his Majesty with such impetuous affection and impatience of delay even in those . . . who must needs know that an abatement of their particular interest would follow?" His answer was that such men had "a clear knowledge and foresight that all would run to rack and ruin unless the public state did settle upon a national bottom." Lord Mordaunt in October 1659 foresaw, as the only alternatives to the rapid return of the King, either "the extirpation of the nobility and gentry . . . or a commonwealth, the Presbyterians included."[2] *A Discourse for a King and Parliament,* a pamphlet of 1660, added that in a republic the gentry must be "reduced to the condition of the vulgar." The crucial moment, Clarendon tells us, came when control of the militia[3] was taken away from "sectaries, persons of no degree and quality" and restored to "the nobility and principal gentry throughout the kingdom." The latter had plenty of reason to rejoice, having restored the King, as Ralph Josselin put it, "out of love to themselves, not him."

Charles was restored not by popular clamour but by the men of property; by Monck, the one general who could pay his troops, acting in close co-operation with the City of Lon-

2. *A Collection of Original Letters and Papers,* ed. T. Carte, 2 vols. (London: Society for the Encouragement of Learning, 1739), II, 230.

3. For the militia, see p. 20 below.

don. The rumps of beef roasted in the streets to celebrate the end of the Rump of the Long Parliament were paid for by rich citizens, and their money was well spent. Clarendon, now Lord Chancellor in the restoration government, told Parliament in 1661 "it is the privilege, . . . the prerogative of the common people of England to be represented by the greatest and learnedest and wealthiest and wisest persons that can be chosen out of the nation; and the confounding the Commons of England . . . with the common people of England was the first ingredient into that accursed dose, . . . a Commonwealth."[4] Clarendon was nearly echoing what Commissary-General Ireton had told the Agitators in the debates at Putney fourteen years earlier: that the rank and file had fought not for the vote, not for a share in running the country, but to have the benefit of laws made by their betters in parliament. Former Parliamentarians and former Cavaliers now spoke the same language against the radicals; and so did Charles II himself: "Without the safety and dignity of the monarchy, neither religion nor property can be preserved." Twenty years earlier defence of "religion and property" had been the slogan of Charles I's opponents.

But why the House of Lords, as well as the monarchy? Here is the Earl of Shaftesbury, ex-Cromwellian, in Harringtonian vein:[5] "There is no prince that ever governed without a nobility or an army. If you will not have the one, you must have the other, or the monarchy cannot long support or keep itself from tumbling into a democratical republic." By the end of the sixteen-fifties the Army had become too expensive and too difficult to control: so the men of property moved over to what Shaftesbury saw as the only alternative if "a democratical republic" was to be avoided.

4. *Parliamentary History,* IV, 205.
5. For Harrington, see pp. 20–21 and 44–45 below.

Why bishops? Richard Baxter, staunch Parliamentarian and enemy of episcopacy, told the House of Commons in his *Sermon of Repentance* in April 1660: "The question is not whether bishops or no, but whether discipline or none." It seemed to this genuinely good and courageous man inevitable that theological convictions should give way to social imperatives. The Earl of Clarendon was understandably reluctant to withdraw the English garrisons from Scotland; he finally yielded only on condition that episcopacy be established there instead. Bishops commanded what a royalist divine called "the King's spiritual militia."[6]

Nor should we underestimate the effectiveness of the deliberate propaganda of the Anglican church, once it had been restored to its monopoly position. "People," King Charles the Martyr had observed, "are governed by the pulpit more than the sword in time of peace"; and the Church of England did its best. January 30, the anniversary of Charles I's execution, became the occasion for sermons in every parish on the duties of subordination and submission. When the rebel Duke of Monmouth claimed in 1685 to die a protestant of the Church of England, a divine said to him on the scaffold: "My Lord, if you be of the Church of England, you must acknowledge the doctrine of non-resistance to be true." For twenty-five years parsons throughout the kingdom had thundered against resistance to the Lord's Anointed. The widely read Anglican *The Whole Duty of Man* told the poor "to be content with whatever entertainment thou findest here [on earth], knowing thou art upon thy journey to a place of infinite happiness, which will make an abundant amends for all the uneasiness and hardship thou canst suffer in the way."

The nonconformist John Bunyan echoed the sentiment:

6. [W. Chestlin], *Persecutio Undecima* (London, 1681), p. 4. First published 1648.

Jesus Christ is "preparing of mansion-houses for those of his poor ones that are now by his enemies kicked to and fro, like footballs in the world, and is not this a blessed sight?" That is a far cry from the Digger Gerrard Winstanley's denunciation of priests in 1652, who "tell the poor people that they must be content with their poverty, and that they shall have their heaven hereafter." Why, Winstanley had asked, "may not we have our heaven here (that is, a comfortable livelihood in the earth), and heaven hereafter too?" "While men are gazing up to heaven, imagining after a happiness or fearing a hell after they are dead," he exploded in words that anticipate Marx, "their eyes are put out, that they see not what is their birth-rights, and what is to be done by them here on earth while they are living." One sees the advantage to the rich of the restoration of episcopacy and an ecclesiastical censorship in 1660, and of the abandonment of politics by the dissenting sects.

Yet in the panic of 1659–60 the pendulum swung too far. The savage legislation of the Clarendon Code expelled opponents of the monarchy (and of the gentry) from their natural strongholds, the government of the boroughs; and forced underground the sectarian congregations from which the main strength of the revolutionaries had come in the preceding two decades. The organization of petitions by the lower orders was prohibited. The Act of Settlement of 1662 authorized J.P.s to drive back to his native parish any person who lacked visible means of support. A rigid censorship ended the relative freedom of political discussion which had existed in the sixteen-forties and had been regained in 1659.

Nevertheless the Revolution left its mark on men's minds. Charles II's reign was dated from his father's death on 30 January 1649; but what had happened between then and 1660 could not be forgotten. Those years had shown that government could be carried on successfully without and even against King, House of Lords, and bishops. The republic's foreign

14

policy had been infinitely more impressive than the monarchy's. Republicanism by 1660 was no longer merely an academic speculation. A rude and vigorous opposition to monarchy was expressed in an unmistakably popular idiom. "What's ado here to bring home a bastard?" asked a Londoner with reference to the return of his most sacred majesty. "Stay! The rogue is not yet come over," added a Lincolnshire man. A glazier of Wapping "would run his knife into [the King] to kill him." Yorkshire yeomen in the early sixteen-sixties observed that "Cromwell and Ireton were as good as the King." "All is traitors that do fight for the King." A Newcastle man was "ready to pull the King's skin over his ears." Another would cut him "as small as herbs in a pot." The nation was less united than the myth suggests. Such remarks survive only by accident: we do not know whether there was a large iceberg of which we can see only the tip.[7]

7. For these and other examples, see my *The World Turned Upside Down*, Penguin edition, p. 354.

III

THERE WAS, then, in 1660 an overwhelming reaction; but the pendulum swung back not to 1640 but to 1641 (or 1646 if Charles I had accepted the terms offered by Parliament then). And, savage though the terror was after 1660, there must have been many survivors from those who had tried to turn the world upside down between 1646 and 1660. What happened to them?

We do not know. Some emigrated, to the West Indies, to New England, to the continent. Others remained with the radical religious sects, which were depoliticized after 1660. George Fox, who in 1657 had rebuked the English Army for not sacking Rome, led the Quakers to pacifism and withdrawal from politics. Other sects followed suit, deciding that Christ's kingdom is not of this world. But the potentiality of revolution was very much present (or at least believed to be present) throughout the period 1660 to 1689. James II ran away too easily in 1688; but the popular movement led by Shaftesbury in 1679 had revived fears of a return of 1641. It was the isolation and defeat of the radicals in Monmouth's rebellion of 1685 which minimized the risk of renewed social upheaval when James II was overthrown.

What the men of property remembered was the New Model Army, which the radicals nearly captured in 1647–49, and which even in the relatively conservative hands of Cromwell and his generals abolished monarchy and House of Lords, extruded the "natural rulers" from control of the counties, from control of the militia, from control of taxation, threatened tithes and other forms of property. Army mutinies had occurred before. They were almost necessary to the running of the Spanish army, parallel to the royal bankruptcies which caused them. But they had no programme which linked them with a civilian party, as the New Model Army Agitators had been linked with the Levellers in 1647, challenging the foundations of society. The Spanish armies had to keep society going in order to get paid.[1]

The English Army had got out of hand in 1647 because it was unpaid. It was brought under control again because land confiscations and the land tax provided the money from which it could be paid. In 1657 Cromwell's reconciliation with the "natural rulers" involved an agreement (in the Humble Petition and Advice) that there should be no land tax. But after his death in 1658 there was talk of renewed confiscations, and this helped to produce the tax strike which in 1660 as in 1640 brought the government down. In 1660 the only alternative to Army rule seemed to be to restore authority to Cavaliers and bishops.

So the political thinking of late seventeenth-century England was dominated by questions of power, of military force. From 1639 to 1689 there was no longer the ruling-class consensus which in the last resort had governed Tudor England. This fact was bound to affect men's thinking, perhaps even before 1639. One of the interesting and unexplained questions of the sixteen-twenties is the feeling which many men expressed, that the lower orders were ripe for revolt if their betters would give them a lead. Such anxieties were outspoken during the clothing depression of the early twenties, and the temptation to the opposition to take advantage of this situation increased with the shame of English non-intervention on the protestant

---

1. Geoffrey Parker, *The Army of Flanders and the Spanish Road, 1567–1659*, (Cambridge: Cambridge University Press, 1972), p. 187 and *passim*.

side in the Thirty Years War. Sir Robert Cotton's *Dangers wherein the Kingdom Standeth and the Remedies,* widely circulated in manuscript before it was printed in 1628, warned that if Parliament pushed its case against the Duke of Buckingham too hard it might unleash a revolt by "the loose and needy multitude, . . . with a glorious pretence of religion and the public safety." Hence, he argued, the attack on the favourite must be prevented, and everything done to convert him to the reformation of grievances and support of Parliament. This attitude perhaps helps to explain the shift of allegiance by Sir Thomas Wentworth and William Noy after 1628, from opposition to government service. In 1630 the funeral sermon on the third Earl of Pembroke—an opposition peer—spoke of the dangers of a civil war which might make possible a Spanish invasion.

In the sixteen-twenties and early thirties caution prevailed. What made revolution possible in 1640 was the Scottish army which had invaded the North of England. Once the Treaty of Ripon had ensured its continuing presence there the reins could be let loose in confidence that our brethren of Scotland would in the last resort prevent social revolt from going too far. So we get the extraordinary scenes of 1640–42, when the gentlemen leaders of the House of Commons and their clerical allies almost encouraged London mobs and anti-Catholic mobs, turned a blind eye to anti-enclosure riots, called on the lower classes to fight against Antichrist, confident that they would remain under the control of their betters.[2]

And indeed, at the crucial moment of the war, in 1644, the Scots army did come into England again, and became the buttress of conservatism. Things went wrong only because the Scottish army made itself infernally unpopular, and because

2. For Antichrist, see pp. 57–60 below.

Parliament, in its anxiety to reduce taxation as soon as the King was beaten (and to get the King into its own hands) paid off the Scots and sent them home before disbanding the New Model Army. From that fatal error (from the point of view of the "natural rulers") all the other unpleasant consequences of the Revolution followed—though Cromwell might well retort that the lower classes never really got out of control even so.

In 1659–60 the situation of 1639–40 repeated itself: refusal of taxes was again possible because there existed General George Monck's paid and disciplined army in the North to guarantee the maintenance of order. Charles II and James II managed throughout their reigns to retain some armed force. In 1688–89 the same effect was attained by William III bringing over with him a professional army to ensure both that James II put up no resistance and that there was no "anarchy." As we know, William succeeded in both. His success throws light on the failures of the movement to exclude the Catholic Duke of York from the succession in 1679–81 and of Monmouth's rebellion in 1685. As late as the end of 1687 Burnet wrote that "a rebellion of which [William] should not retain the command would certainly establish a commonwealth." Almanacs in 1687 and 1688 were discussing the advantages of a republic.[3] There were riots and plunder in the winter of 1688–89, in London and other cities.

Henceforth 1688 was eulogized as the revolution to end revolutions: and hatred of standing armies reached pathological proportions among the English propertied classes. Cromwell's use of the Army in the fifties to suppress the radicals and to expel the Rump of the Long Parliament made it as unpopular with republicans as with conservatives; and James II's army

3. Bernard Capp, *Astrology and the Popular Press: English Almanacs, 1500–1800* (London and Boston: Faber and Faber, 1979), p. 96.

aroused intense anxiety in 1687–88 among Tories as well as Whigs, both by its own suspect radical inclinations and because it enabled the King to supplant the "natural rulers" and hand local government over to former republicans. Suspicion of his army was undoubtedly one of the explanations of James II's failure to achieve an effective alliance of extreme right and extreme left, catholics and radical dissenters, against the "natural rulers." Henceforth professional armies are regarded with grave suspicion by the whole political nation.

Against standing armies patriotic Englishmen of property extolled the militia and the navy. The militia, officered by the gentry, was the army of property, from whose ranks the lowest classes were excluded. It was described in 1645 as "the fortress of liberty."[4] It played a part in the restoration of Charles II in 1660: its defection to William of Orange in most areas was decisive in 1688.

Against this background the political theory of Thomas Hobbes perhaps acquires a new immediacy, with its emphasis on naked force or power. For Hobbes the protection which the sovereign gave to his subjects was the sole and sufficient justification of his power: it was silly to bother about the "legitimacy" of any sovereign who gave protection. Against this hardheaded realism the only valid critique is that of James Harrington, an admirer of Hobbes: "As he said of the law, that without this sword it is but paper; so he might have thought of this sword, that without a hand it is but cold iron. . . . But an army is a beast that has a great belly, and must be fed; wherefore this will come to what pastures you have, and what pas-

---

4. *Thurloe State Papers*, ed. T. Birch, 7 vols. (London, 1742), I, 54; cf. Marvell:
        Unhappy! shall we never more
        That sweet militia restore
        When gardens only had their towers
        And all the garrisons were flowers.
        (*Upon Appleton House*)

tures you have will come to the balance of property, without which the public sword is but a name or mere spitfrog."

In the late sixteen-forties and early fifties Anthony Ascham and others anticipated Hobbes's *Leviathan* in abandoning the concept of "legitimacy" as the justification of political authority, and concentrating upon *de facto* power and ability to afford protection to the subjects who lived under this power. Some historians recently seem to me to have exaggerated the importance of this group of thinkers, which includes John Dury, Francis Rous, and Marchamont Nedham as well as Ascham. Their brief vogue owed less to the intrinsic intellectual merits of the theorists than to the fashion which prevailed twenty years ago for proclaiming the end of ideology. The main interest of Ascham and his like, as of the end-of-ideology school, lies in what both groups tell us about the world in which they wrote. In the early sixteen-fifties there seems to have been a weariness, a suspicion of ideological politics, a desire to escape from previous commitments and loyalties, a willingness to withdraw from opposition to the all-powerful Army even if not giving its rule enthusiastic support. In such a climate, it was pleasant to be reminded by the impeccably pious Dury that St. Paul had said that the powers that be are ordained of God—all powers, however they got there; or to have Ascham's or Nedham's more sophisticated arguments for accepting the inevitable. These theorists also show how the ground was prepared for *Leviathan,* published in 1651.[5] The other writers cannot compare with Hobbes in originality or depth. But they do help to show the immediate relevance of Hobbes's demonstration that protection rather than legitimacy was the significant justification of the sovereign. Hobbes himself claimed that *Le-*

5. Q. Skinner, "The Ideological Context of Hobbes's Political Thought," *Historical Journal* 9 (1966): 286–317; "Conquest and Consent: Thomas Hobbes and the Engagement Controversy," in G. E. Aylmer, ed., *The Interregnum: The Quest for Settlement, 1646–1660* (London: Macmillan, 1972), pp. 79–98.

viathan helped to persuade ex-royalists to accept the Commonwealth, and he may well have been right. The other pamphleteers show that such justifications were in demand. They were no doubt useful again in 1660, as in 1688.[6]

6. G. M. Straka, *The Anglican Reaction to the Revolution of 1688* (Madison, Wis.: State Historical Society, 1962), *passim*.

IV

SO THE HERITAGE of the English Revolution differed greatly
from that of the French Revolution (and the Russian), especially in relation to the army. Thanks to the coincidence of the
Thirty Years War with the English Revolution, and to the
speed with which Charles II was rushed home after the Peace
of the Pyrenees had ended war between France and Spain in
1659, there was no foreign military intervention on behalf of
the Stuarts, consequently no revolutionary wars of liberation.
The Cromwellian conquest of Scotland in 1650–52 perhaps
presents some analogies with the operations of the French revolutionary armies in the Rhineland and in Italy in the
seventeen-nineties, but Cromwell's maintenance of English
liberty in Ireland was anything but liberating for the Irish.
There was a lot of international talk in the forties and fifties,
but the Rump's Dutch war (1652–54), like the conquest of
Ireland, was all too clearly motivated by strategy and economics rather than by ideology: and when in the sixteen-nineties
England and the Netherlands found themselves at last in alliance it was forty years too late. England still might just have
led a protestant crusade in the early fifties; but William III's
wars against Louis XIV were nationalist, not ideological. The
Williamite conquest of Ireland confirmed the Cromwellian
settlement.

Cromwell, like Stalin and Mao, pursued a policy of revolution in one country. Protestant ideology was ignored when the
enemy was the Netherlands, remembered in Ireland and against
France and Spain. In the name of protestantism Ireland was

economically enslaved, and bases in the West Indies for trade in African Negroes were won. There is a terrible symbolic significance here. So England—unlike France and the U.S.S.R.— never had permanent conscript armies. There was no tradition of revolutionary wars of liberation; to fight her wars England hired foreign mercenaries, or press-ganged the unemployed, thus serving two useful purposes. The act of 1708 providing for conscription made it clear that only those with "no lawful calling or employment" were to be taken: through friendly J.P.s employers were able to use the threat of call-up against recalcitrant workers.

There is another paradox about the Army—its relation to religious toleration. Toleration established itself in England in the forties because the Army wanted it—and virtually no one else in the political nation did. Any free Parliament, from the Long Parliament through the Protectorate Parliaments to the Cavalier Parliament of 1661–79, wanted to persecute those who challenged the state church. During the Revolution radical protestantism established itself too strongly in the towns for even the Clarendon Code to wipe it out, but that Code did restore the dominance of parson and squire in the countryside. Charles II could never win toleration for Roman Catholics and protestant non-conformists because he had no army adequate for the purpose. James II failed because his army was papist, and so he could not win the confidence of protestant dissenters. The grudging Toleration Act of 1689 gave liberty of worship to protestant dissenters in towns, but at the price of their continued exclusion from politics, and of the continuance of gentry control over their villages. It recognized a real balance of forces: the strength of organized urban dissent made a genuine national church impossible, but equally the existence of urban dissent made the church necessary for the squires. The Toleration Act accepted this balance: nonconformity did not seriously penetrate most rural areas until Wesleyanism in the eighteenth century—and then dissent was perhaps only following industry.

I have been foreshortening, of course. One of the interesting consequences of the survival of the aristocracy is the survival of military values. Spokesmen of the defeated royalists laid great stress on honour and the military virtues. As Sir William Davenant put it, "The most effectual schools of morality are courts and camps," from which he took his recommended patterns of behaviour. "Courts form'd . . . war . . . to tame the rude."[1] This is one aspect of the fashion for heroic drama: we may compare the revival of duelling under Charles II. Cromwell in the fifties was consciously trying to cash in on royalist militarism: he used Davenant to make propaganda for his war against Spain, in *The Cruelty of the Spaniards in Peru* and *The History of Sir Francis Drake*. When I wrote a book on Oliver Cromwell I quoted four poets—Waller, Marvell, Dryden, and Sprat—on how Cromwell showed "the ancient way of conquering abroad"; "once more joined us to the continent"; "taught the English lion how to roar." I then noticed that not one of the four had supported Parliament in the forties, and that three of them were to be enthusiastic monarchists after the restoration. In fact it was this aspect of Oliver's rule that was especially remembered in court circles during the inglorious days of Charles II. "Everybody," Pepys tells us in 1667, "do nowadays reflect upon Oliver and commend him, what brave things he did and made all the neighbour princes fear him."

It is arguable that in the eighteenth century England was the most aggressively bellicose nation in Europe, its symbol John Bull with his cudgel. But hatred of standing armies, together with the growing wealth of England, meant that this

---

1. Sir William Davenant, *Gondibert*, ed. D. F. Gladish (Oxford: Clarendon Press, 1971), pp. 12–13, 263.

aggressive policy was pursued by navies and by hiring the troops of other nations when fighting was required on the continent of Europe or in India. The modern navy dates from the Commonwealth. Even William the Liberator could not persuade his subjects to allow him the army he wanted, but Parliament was always generous in providing for the navy. This was one of the many advantages which Britain derived from being an island: a navy cannot be used for internal policing. The navy ensured England's dominance in the markets of America and Asia, and ultimately won her a virtual monopoly of the African slave trade. Unlike the poverty-stricken Scots and Irish gentry, English gentlemen no longer needed to take up mercenary military service on the continent, as they had done in large numbers in the late sixteenth and early seventeenth centuries. There were now enough jobs for them at home—in trade, in the civil service, in the navy. It was in the years after 1688 that gentlemen stopped wearing swords.

A final paradox. I argued that in the fifties the alternatives were an army, or a restoration of King, House of Lords, bishops: and that the latter trio were restored in the interests of trade, property, and social stability. Yet the foreign policy of the Protectorate was continued. The bill of 1661 annexing Cromwell's conquests of Dunkirk and Jamaica had "the most universal consent and approbation from the whole nation that ever any bill could be attended with."[2] Yet, looked at merely from the point of view of carrying out a commercial foreign policy, many shrewd observers agreed in rating a republic higher than monarchy. Cardinal Mazarin in 1646 said that an English republic would be "an evil without comparison for France," in view of the financial strength of any country where

2. C. M. Andrews, *The Colonial Period of American History: The Settlements* (New Haven: Yale University Press, 1964), III, 32. First published 1937.

taxes were paid by consent.[3] Such reasoning became a radical commonplace. "Democracy," wrote the Harringtonian Henry Neville in 1681, "is much more powerful than aristocracy, because the latter cannot arm the people for fear they should seize upon the government." He prudently used the safe example of Athens to argue that conquests are best made by a popular government. Henry Moyle a couple of decades later insisted that the Roman republic showed the inferiority of kingly governments in making conquests.[4] In 1660 a sacrifice of power in foreign affairs had been made in the interests of internal stability and the authority of the gentry. But after 1688 and the foundation of the Bank of England in 1694 the English constitution combined the financial advantages of a republic with the social advantages of monarchy. It was a very happy compromise for those at the top.

Yet we must never forget the strength of monarchy's appeal to ordinary people, which is one of the most difficult things for us to grasp about the collapse of the English republic. We read the Levellers, Winstanley, Hobbes, Milton, Harrington, all of whom discuss politics in rational intellectual terms. Then we are faced with the fact that *Eikon Basilike, the Pourtraicture of His Sacred Majestie in His Solitudes and Sufferings,* outsold all of them put together, fraudulent though it is, exposed though it had been by Milton among others. We tend to forget the still surviving magical aura of kingship, as we forget that the seventeenth century was still, for the mass of men and women, a pre-rational age. The royal touch which cured scrofula (TB glands in the neck) was a relic of age-old royal healing powers. Charles II started touching in exile immediately after his father's execution; people suffering from scrofula apparently

3. *Recueil des instructions données aux ambassadeurs et ministres de France,* ed. J. J. Jusserand, vol. 24, *Angleterre* (Paris: E. de Boccard, 1929), i, *(1648–65),* pp. 35–38.

4. For this use of ancient history, see p. 46 below.

went abroad to be touched, which suggests that the well-to-do believed no less than the populace. In 1660 the Merrie Monarch touched 260 at Breda before taking ship for England; he is alleged to have touched over 92,000 persons during his reign. James II naturally did a lot of touching. William III was sceptical, but Anne—the last Stuart—was the last English sovereign to exercise the healing power, touching Dr. Johnson (unsuccessfully) in 1712.

A holy, magic-making sovereign appeared to be above the mere political struggle, and so was of inestimable value to those who controlled him. In 1647 General Ireton told the captive Charles I that he had more need of the Army than they had of him. In the short run Ireton was right. Charles was executed, the generals ran the country. But in the long run the royal martyr was stronger than the generals, magic stronger even than the sword. A King was needed as the keystone of the arch of social inequality. But in the longest run of all, the lesson was learnt that the magic could be controlled. "What we need is a King with plenty of holy oil about him," wrote a correspondent of the Earl of Manchester in 1659. The age of magic is over, the age of consciously manipulated monarchy has arrived. By the mid-eighteenth century David Hume thought claims to divine right laughable. Yet even under the Hanoverians—no magic makers—it was still important for the ruling class that belief in the dignity and uniqueness of the king should be maintained. As Gibbon put it, "The good of society is interested in every institution which tends to inspire reverence and awe for the supreme magistrate. The laws of England have not only vested their king with very extensive powers, but they likewise attribute to him several high perfections and attributes inherent to his political character though often very foreign to his personal one."[5]

5. Edward Gibbon, *English Essays*, ed. P. B. Craddock (Oxford: Clarendon Press, 1972), pp. 69–70.

V

So, TO SUM UP, the apparent similarity between the England
of 1640 and the England of 1660 is illusory. The institutions are
the same—monarchy, House of Lords, House of Commons,
episcopal state church, common law; but the social context has
changed. The prerogative courts, which made it possible for
Charles I to aspire to an absolute monarchy with episcopal support, have been abolished. The House of Commons is indubi-
tably the more important of the two Houses of Parliament,
and in the last resort its will must prevail over crown and
church alike. In Harringtonian terms, the King of England has
ceased to be a monarch and has become "a prince in a commonwealth."

But among the political consequences of the Revolution I
would stress that as the power of the House of Commons increased, so its representative character declined. The attempted
incursion of the people and even the poor into politics in the
mid-seventeenth century boomeranged. Fear of radical change
meant that until the nineteenth century there was no redistri-
bution or extension of the franchise, such as the Levellers had
demanded and as had been partially implemented in the Instrument of Government in 1653.[1] The law of debt remained unre-
formed; of the many other legal reforms called for by the radicals, the only ones ultimately implemented were in spheres like
Habeas Corpus and the independence of juries, which affected
the men of property. It seemed safer to stick to the old law,

1. See p. 9 above.

with all its irrational anomalies, around which money could always find a way, than to tamper with the law which guaranteed property. For now the property of the well-to-do was safe from any threat from the executive; Parliament, representing the "natural rulers," was now the lawmaker; and from 1701 judges became responsible to it, not to the executive. Meanwhile borough electorates were deliberately narrowed by the House of Commons, which before 1640 had been in favour of widening them. In 1740 the Commons represented a significantly smaller proportion of the population than had been the case in 1640. Smaller electorates were easier to corrupt as well as easier to manage; anyone rich enough could buy himself into Parliament if he wanted to. Corruption became a national sport, demoralizing the bribers as well as the bribed. It took a great deal of middle-class austerity in the nineteenth century to get rid of it.

When Parliament was restored in 1660 it at once recalled Charles II: there was apparently no talk of a republic in parliamentary circles in 1688. The aristocracy's restoration in 1660 ensured some survival of respect for the military virtues, notwithstanding the well-orchestrated hatred of standing armies. Officering the amateur militia remained the outward visible sign of the gentry's power, based ultimately on the military force of the armigerous class. Their privileges were also enshrined in the game laws, in the right to hunt over other people's land. Parliament authorized *game-keepers* to enter the houses of the lower classes to search for weapons. Only the upper-class Englishman's house was his castle. Levellers and Diggers, who had wished to see the whole people armed, were forgotten.

Milton referred in 1660 to the "vain and groundless apprehension that nothing but kingship can restore trade." Monarchy and House of Lords returned to protect business men no less than the gentry. There was a division of labour. Gentle-men controlled the villages, but—especially after 1688 and 1694 —foreign policy was determined by commercial interests. The conflict between the landed and monied interests, of which Swift made so much, was in the last resort shadowboxing.

We should not underestimate the long-term consequences for English social and intellectual history of the survival of aris-tocracy and gentry. Many traditional values were preserved— much more than in France or Germany where revolutions came later. The first country to modernize has today become almost the least modernized of all west European countries. When after the Industrial Revolution social mobility could no longer be contained, when in the nineteenth century the mid-dle class was at last enfranchised, the public schools trained the sons of this class to accept a great part of the aristocratic ethos. The public schools now form the last ditch of conservatism in England. When a Frenchman addresses another Frenchman as "Monsieur," he is proclaiming human equality; when an En-glishman addresses another Englishman as "Sir" he is either in-sulting him or toadying to him.

Manipulated monarchy, I suggested, was one heritage of the Revolution; manipulated crowds were another. In 1647 London mobs were used against the Independents and against the Army. Shaftesbury and his City allies used crowds at the time of the Popish Plot; church and King mobs appeared in the Sacheverell riots of 1709 and continued at least until the Gor-don riots of 1780 and the rabbling of dissenters in the age of the French Revolution. The Whig oligarchy had indeed noth-ing to offer the disenfranchised. Like the Irish, the English common people were excluded from the pale of the constitu-tion, and as we have seen, this pale was narrowing from the second half of the seventeenth century. There was a genuine lower-class Toryism, which could be incited against dissenters or against the Voluntary Societies which tried to interfere with the simple pleasures of the poor.[2] And in the villages there was a conscious "cakes and ale" paternalism, exemplified by Addison's Sir Roger de Coverley, a nostalgia for a traditional Merrie England which the upper and lowest classes shared in their mutual hostility to sordid urban pettifoggying. Hence the propaganda importance of exaggerating in retrospect the killjoy activities of Cromwell's Major-Generals and Puritans generally, a legend which has proved remarkably tenacious. In fact the Major-Generals were mainly influenced by security considerations when they put down horse-racing and bear-baiting in the sixteen-fifties; the activities which probably most enraged the "natural rulers" were the Major-Generals' attempts to get embezzled local endowments restored to the relief of the poor for which they had been established.

Contemplating the political consequences of the fact that the English Revolution was so much less radical than the French, Russian, and Chinese Revolutions, some historians have developed a greater interest in the defeated left wing of the English revolutionaries—in Levellers who were remembered by eighteenth- and nineteenth-century radicals, and in Diggers who were forgotten. In the sixteen-fifties the phrase "the common man" was already being used defensively. The astrologer William Lilly spoke of "the woeful condition of the common man," everyone "labouring to enrich himself and posterity by the sweat and labour of the common man." Historians still have not altogether liberated themselves from the propagandist assumptions of seventeenth-century Tories and nineteenth-century Whigs about the common people in the seventeenth century. Winstanley's claim that they were "part of the nation" was soon forgotten. But he was, after all, right: and when we ask ourselves what has gone wrong with En-

2. For the Voluntary Societies, see p. 69 below.

gland in the past three centuries, one part of the answer is that the arrogant self-confidence of a ruling class enjoying an unprecedented security and prosperity was for too long unchecked by any need to pay serious attention to the views of those beneath them.

Once the historical event has taken place, it appears inevitable; alternatives recede. History is written by winners, especially the history of revolutions. It is nevertheless worth trying to penetrate imaginatively back to the time when options seemed open. It would be nice to think that the old cynicism "the only lesson of history is that the lessons of history are never learnt" need not always be true.

VI

I HAVE ARGUED ELSEWHERE that the main long-term significance of the English Revolution was neither constitutional nor
political nor religious but economic. In trade and agriculture it
cleared the way for the capitalist development which made it
possible for England to become the country of the first Industrial Revolution.[1]

I hope I do not need to labour the point that this outcome
was far from the intentions of most if not all of the revolutionaries. I have my reservations about the phrase "the Puritan Revolution," but few would deny that the main ideological driving
force in the Revolution was religious. Yet what emerged from
twenty years of strife was not the kingdom of God but a world
safe for business men to make profits in, ensured not only by
the overthrow of the old régime but also by the defeat of the
radical revolutionaries, divided as they were among themselves. The men who took over in the sixteen-fifties, the men
who made the restoration, were the "realists," their main concern to preserve property and social subordination.

They probably did not contemplate the full consequences of
the society which they created, or consolidated. The abolition
of feudal tenures (1646, confirmed in 1660) gave landowners
absolute property in their estates, freed from arbitrary death
duties and dependence on the crown: this made possible long-

1. See my "A Bourgeois Revolution?" in J. G. A. Pocock, ed., *Three British
Revolutions: 1641, 1688, 1776* (Princeton University Press, 1980).

term planning and capital investment. The radical demand for equivalent security of tenure for copyholders was specifically rejected in the act of 1660; on the contrary, an act of 1677 made the property of small freeholders no less insecure than that of copyholders except in the unlikely case that it was supported by written title. Together these provisions ensured the triumph of capitalist farming in England—"a new chapter in the history of the (rural) world," Le Roy Ladurie called it.

The consequent agricultural boom of the late-seventeenth and eighteenth centuries solved the food problem caused by the sixteenth and early seventeenth century expansion of England's population. England became a corn-exporting country, and agriculture became the country's greatest capitalist industry. The total standard of living rose. But the profits of this boom went to the rich. The poor were dispossessed or forced into wage labour. This contributed to the decline in the size of the Parliamentary electorate, and enhanced the control over it of the well-to-do. Gregory King's table of 1696 suggests that paupers and wage-labourers may have amounted to half the population. They were wholly dependent on their social superiors, incapable of political independence. In the eighteenth century they would be called the mob.

The 1662 Act of Settlement ended the mobile existence of those squatters who had previously been, in Gerrard Winstanley's words, "out of sight or out of slavery." He had had a very different vision of communal cultivation of commons, wastes, and forests by the poor in order to put an end to begging. The defeat of the radicals in the Revolution marked the end of the relative democracy of English village communities. One sees perhaps why the free land still available in America, with no manor courts and dues, no tithes, no compulsion to wage labour, was attractive enough to make men and women risk the appalling hazards of the Atlantic crossing and of pioneering in the wilderness. It offered the only social revolution now possible, a refuge for the more enterprising among the discontented, and so a safety-valve.[2]

Confirmation of the Commonwealth's Navigation Act at the restoration and its enforcement in two more wars against the Dutch, thanks to the great fleet built up during the revolutionary decades, established a closed imperial market, and led to what Professor Davis has called the "Commercial Revolution." English merchants bought colonial goods cheap and sold them dear—a double monopoly. Shipping and the reexport trades boomed. The tonnage passing through the port of London doubled between 1640 and 1680. The profits of this monopoly of imperial trade were founded largely on slavery; this cannot too often be emphasized, in view especially of the coy silence of many orthodox economic historians on the subject. From the sixteen-forties Barbados and other West Indian islands switched over to large-scale sugar production, manned almost exclusively by slave labour. Cromwell's conquest of Jamaica in 1655 offered a secure base for the slave traders in the heart of the Indies, from which they could sell illegally to Spanish America as well as legally to the English islands. By the end of the century English merchants were supplying all Europe with sugar and tobacco from the West Indies as well as with calico, silks, and pepper from the Far East.

The system also stimulated production of consumer goods in England, both for the closed market of the American colonies and for use in exchange for slaves in Africa. Customs revenue leapt forward. By 1700 it was ten times what it had been a century earlier. Not the least of the crimes of the Stuart monarchs was their lack of enthusiam for trade and the colonies. James II doubled the tax on sugar in Barbados, ousted the

2. Cf. Sumner C. Powell, *Puritan Village: The Formation of a New England Town* (New York: Anchor Books, 1965), pp. 107–8, 132–34, 182–84.

36

planters from government, and sold seats on the Barbados Council. After 1688 the monopoly of the Royal African Company was broken, and freedom led to a rapid expansion of the slave trade. The War of Spanish Succession won for the English merchants the Asiento, a monopoly of supplying slaves to the whole Spanish American empire—beyond the wildest dreams of John Hawkins a century and a half earlier. The Commercial Revolution stimulated English industrial development; the monopoly imperial market led to an accumulation of capital: both were necessary pre-conditions for the Industrial Revolution which made England the workshop of the world.[3]

In thinking about the long-term consequences of the English Revolution it is difficult to over-estimate the effects of the slave trade, whose virtual monopoly was ultimately secured for English merchants thanks to the state power which this Revolution had so greatly enhanced. English planters did not settle in the West Indies (or in India), as they did in New England: they made their pile as quickly as possible and came back to set themselves up as landowners in England. The former slave-owners brought with them a contempt for the labour force which made their profits, and this must have influenced intellectual attitudes in England, just entering on the Industrial Revolution. Even professional do-gooders like the Society for the Propagation of the Gospel owned slaves in the West Indies, and did not allow them to be instructed in Christianity lest they should get ideas above their station. So the slave trade must have accentuated the Puritan tendency to hypocrisy, to double-thinking, which was to be so conspicuous among pious nineteenth-century factory-owners. Slavers and slave owners, and crews of ships from Bristol and Liverpool, whose prosperity was based largely on the slave trade, cannot but have regarded

3. R. Davis, *A Commercial Revolution*, Historical Association Pamphlet (London, 1967), *passim*.

human life and suffering as unimportant where money was to be made. This brutalization must have reflected back on the mother-country. Signs of a colour bar begin to appear in English literature during the seventeenth century. At the beginning of the century Othello and Pocahontas are treated as human beings; by the end Thomas Rymer is rebuking Shakespeare for showing so little colour prejudice.

What is interesting is that the opponents of slavery seem to come from the Tory ranks: the Whigs, originally the libertarians, more and more succumbed to the market and the monied interest. It was the Tory Aphra Behn who denounced slavery and glorified the noble savage in *Oroonoko* (1688, but probably written some twenty years earlier). A century later it was Samuel Johnson who raised his glass to "the next insurrection of the negroes in the West Indies," and the Tory Gibbon who noted that the inhabitants of Ghana believed that the slave ships exported Africans to feed "the polite cannibals of Europe." Gibbon commented that "this false suspicion is rather favourable than injurious to Christian humanity"—since the fate which in fact awaited the slaves was worse than being eaten. Gibbon's irony reminds us of that other Tory ironist, Jonathan Swift, whose *Modest Proposal for Preventing the Children of Poor People from being a Burden to their Parents or Country, and for making them beneficial to the Publick* (1729) contained a similar cannibalistic suggestion that the Irish should serve up their children as food for the English, to the advantage of both sides.

The economic triumphs of the seventeenth and eighteenth centuries included the ruthless subjugation and exploitation of the first English colony, Ireland, with consequences that are now coming home to roost. In the home country there was a new hardening of social divisions. The defeat of the radicals in the Revolution ensured the triumph of capitalist agriculture, at the cost of a disruption of traditional ways of life; the home market expanded because of enclosure and the subjugation of men and women to what they regarded as the slavery of wage labour.[4]

The century after the Revolution saw an end of the family farm and the family small business as the economically dominant units. With them went the family partnership of the household, in which the wife had enjoyed some status in subordination to the master of the family. As the workshop was severed from the household, most women became domestic drudges for their absentee wage-earning husbands: for them the factories were not yet liberating. If they offered employment to women it was sweated labour at the lowest rates. Removal of the workshop from the household also divorced middle-class wives from production, from their status as junior partner in the family firm. Instead they read novels, cultivated white hands and the vapours.

Late seventeenth- and eighteenth-century England was a two-class society with a two-class mentality. Part of the strength of Puritanism had been its work ethic, the conviction that it was a duty to God to labour in one's calling. In the household economy, where the family was not only a unit of production but also a little church, a little school, this had a certain reality: the interests of the master of the household and his dependants *were* linked. But first the defeat of Puritanism, then the undermining of the household economy by enclosure and the factories, destroyed this mutuality. Was working to make profits for an absentee landlord or a factory owner really the way to glorify God?

I have no wish to sentimentalize the feudal-patriarchal relations which preceded the rise of capitalism. But what survived of the protestant emphasis on the godliness of labour *after* the dissolution of the household economy was a conviction in the

4. See my *Change and Continuity in Seventeenth-Century England* (London: Weidenfeld and Nicolson, 1974), chap. 10.

minds of the propertied class that poverty was a sin, that enclosure and eviction were good for the poor as well as for enclosers and the national economy. The poor came to be accepted as a permanent part of the population just as the wealth of the country as a whole leapt forward. A series of judicial pronouncements against any restraint on trade helped the rich, long before Adam Smith, to think of laissez-faire as "natural" and therefore divine. This together with slavery led to a contempt for the rights of the labouring people just at a time when they most needed moral support. Machine-breaking and trade unions appeared together as the answer. It was a harsh self-help society, mitigated by sects looking after their own poor,[5] and by some surviving paternalism of the type which Fielding delighted to portray in his novels. Such Squire Westerns were in fact often jealously resentful of newly rich industrialists.

During the Revolution Levellers and other would-be reformers of the law had insisted on the superiority of jurors to judges—on strictly class grounds. Judges were gentlemen, expensively educated at the Inns of Court, jurors were mechanics. But a statute of 1665 said that jurors should possess freehold land worth at least £20 per annum (ten times the Parliamentary franchise); so the famous cases of the restoration period which confirmed the rights of juries did not have the social effect which the Levellers had intended. The laws protecting property became more savage in the late-seventeenth and eighteenth centuries. Again it was the Tory Samuel Johnson who complained in 1751 that the death penalty was imposed for too many and too trivial causes.[6] "Liberty cannot be provided for in a general sense if property be preserved," Ireton had told the Levellers in 1647; history proved him right. The state belonged to those with a permanent fixed interest in land

5. See p. 75 below.
6. *The Rambler,* No. 114.

or in corporations. "The poorer and meaner people," wrote the self-made Duke of Albemarle, "that have no interest in the commonwealth but the use of breath, these are always dangerous to the peace of a kingdom, and having nothing to lose, willingly embrace all means of innovation, in the hope of gaining something by other men's ruin." He thought there were three remedies for this situation—colonization, war, and industrial expansion to create employment.[7] All three were in fact adopted in the century after he wrote.

Taxation mirrored the new social relations. The taxes which had been particularly obnoxious to the monied interest —monopolies, impositions, arbitrary fines—were abolished by the Long Parliament and replaced by taxes voted by Parliament, falling especially on the landed and poorer classes—the land tax and the excise, both inventions of the Revolution. The excise was a tax on consumption, a form of enforced saving: it helped the accumulation of capital. The land tax became permanent only after 1688. With the Glorious Revolution and the foundation of the Bank of England confidence between government and taxpayers (the big ones, at least) was established, making possible a long-term public debt guaranteed by Parliament, something that had not been possible under Charles II and was not possible under Louis XIV of France. The monied interest was no longer a junior partner to the landed interest, which had itself gone over to the new life-style—production for the market, profits invested in the funds. Younger sons of the gentry were set free from the dependence of primogeniture by the opening up of other jobs in which they might get rich quicker than their older brothers—the civil service, the navy, the Army, India, trade.

In France and in the Soviet Union the Revolution com-

7. George Monck, Duke of Albemarle, *Observations upon Military and Political Affairs* (London, 1671), pp. 145–46.

pleted the monarchy's centralizing task. In the English Revolution the parliamentarian armies conquered Wales, the North and South-West, Ireland and Scotland. But centralization was achieved by the dominance of the London market over local monopolies, and by sects centred on London, rather than by a London-based bureaucracy. The culture of London and the home counties gradually spread to the outlying regions, including the Scottish Lowlands—especially after the Union of 1707 revived the Cromwellian union of 1652. But in post-revolutionary England there was no central standing army: internal policing was left to the militia officered by the local rulers; the centralization of the empire to the advantage of London was the affair of the navy.

We do not perhaps reflect sufficiently on the importance of water communications—rivers, and the fact that Britain is an island—in ensuring the economic dominance of London, as earlier they had ensured Amsterdam's supremacy. Capitalist agriculture could be developed best where water communications facilitated the transport of heavy loads: not even the nineteenth-century railways disrupted the old peasant society on the continent to the same extent. Colbert's attempt to push the French economy on to capitalist lines foundered, among other things, on problems of distribution arising from the lack of good internal communications. The French hinterland (with the exception of areas around Marseilles and Bordeaux) was still suffering from severe famines at the end of the seventeenth and the beginning of the eighteenth centuries, at a time when England was immune.[8]

It was natural that England, which in the seventeenth century became the leading capitalist power, should also lead in the beginnings of economic theory. Thomas Mun's *England's*

8. E. W. Fox, *History in Geographic Perspective: The Other France* (New York: Norton, 1972), pp. 86–95 and *passim*.

Treasure by Foreign Trade was premature when he wrote it about 1630; it came into its own when it was published in 1664. Mun and other early admirers of the bourgeois Netherlands slowly extended the idea that there were predictable regularities of economic behaviour which existed in their own right, and that government attempts to control trade or to force it into directions which were "unnatural" were bound to fail. As the market expanded, as more and more of the British Isles was drawn into London's orbit, so the idea of "economic man" gained respectability. Enclosure was defended as economically advantageous to the country as a whole, even (in the long run) to those who might be evicted in the process. As capitalism delivered the goods, a new ethic replaced the older communual ideals which derived from an economy of scarcity. Economic pamphleteers like Sir Josiah Child, Charles Davenant, Nicholas Barbon, Sir Dudley North, assumed that men act rationally with an eye to their own economic interest; by the end of the century the market economy had spread sufficiently widely for this to be true enough for statistical purposes; and the science of economics was born.[9]

Marx rightly called Sir William Petty "the father of political economy." The impetus to his "political arithmetic" seems to have come from surveying conquered Ireland; the science of demography arose from Graunt's study of mortality in the greatest city of Europe. Winstanley, Harrington, and Locke drew on the experiences of the revolutionary decades to evolve theories of the relation of economics to politics, and of the influence of class structures. Such insights contributed to Locke's synthesis, and to eighteenth-century thinkers like Bernard de Mandeville and the Scottish school of sociologists culminating

9. I have drawn on J. O. Appleby, *Economic Thought and Ideology in Seventeenth-Century England* (Princeton University Press, 1978), although this excellent book was published after these lectures were delivered.

in Adam Smith—great both as a political economist and as a sociological historian.

Nor was this the only contribution of the Revolution to historical understanding. Although "providential" theories of history did not lose their vogue, the fact that partisans of both sides in the civil war used such arguments weakened their effectiveness (as against the days when there still had been a consensus among the literate—or when the censorship made it appear that there was a consensus). Both Clarendon and Baxter, for instance, wrote within a framework of divine control of history, yet they were both also acute sociological observers of the events in which they had participated. "Though the immediate finger . . . of God must be acknowledged in these perplexities and distractions," Clarendon explained, "yet he who shall diligently observe the distempers and conjunctures of time, the ambition, pride and folly of persons, and the sudden growth of wickedness, from want of care and circumspection in the first impressions, will find all this bulk of misery to have proceeded, and to have been brought upon us, from the same natural causes and means which have usually attended kingdoms swollen with long plenty, pride and excess."[10] Economic motivation, it is true, was more often attributed to one's enemies than to one's friends (by Thomas Hobbes, Lucy Hutchinson, the Duchess of Newcastle, and Edmund Ludlow, for instance); but again the effect of having more than one interpretation of the same event made the arguments concentrate on secondary causes to an extent hitherto unknown. Specific economic and class analyses like those of Levellers, Diggers, and Harringtonians fortified this tendency towards secularization.

Harrington's ideas became almost orthodox in the later seventeenth century. Power naturally follows property, unless ar-

10. Edward Hyde, Earl of Clarendon, *History of the Rebellion,* ed. W. D. Macray, 6 vols. (Oxford: Clarendon Press, 1888), I, 2.

tificially prevented. Andrew Marvell's much-misunderstood remark that the Parliamentarian cause "was too good to have been fought for" is in fact an urbanely ironical defence of that cause in words that almost echo Harrington: "Men may spare their pains where Nature is at work, and the world will not go the faster for our driving. Even as our present Majesty's happy restoration did itself, all things else happen in their best and proper time, without any need of our officiousness."

In his poems, too, Marvell expressed a sense of destiny which rose above mere theological statement. It was "madness to resist or blame / The force of angry heaven's flame." "Ancient rights" were pleaded in vain against those who ruined "the great work of time." As for Hobbes, what mattered was whether "men are strong or weak." Milton in *Paradise Lost* used the myth of the Fall of Man to account for the failure of the English people to live up to their great historical opportunity; in *Paradise Regained* and *Samson Agonistes* he suggested ways in which good men could both accept and transcend the blind cyclical forces of history. Hobbes, from his very different angle, claimed that "if in time as in place there were degrees of high and low, I verily believe the highest of time would be that which passed betwixt 1640 and 1660."[11]

11. *The English Works of Thomas Hobbes of Malmesbury,* ed. Sir W. Molesworth, 11 vols. (London: J. Bohn, 1839–45), VI, 165.

VII

BEFORE LOOKING at the more specifically intellectual consequences of these political and economic changes, there is one
very elementary point to make, but a point which is often forgotten by those who discuss such matters. The sixteen-forties
and early fifties had been a quite unique period of freedom to
publish. After 1660 as before 1640 there was a very strict censorship. All books on history or politics had to be licensed by
one of Charles II's Secretaries of State, books on divinity, philosophy, or science by the Archbishop of Canterbury, the
Bishop of London, or the Vice-Chancellor of Oxford or Cambridge. (Oxford in 1683 condemned the political writings of
Hobbes, Milton, Baxter, and many others). In the first two
decades after 1660 there were none but official newspapers.
Printing, one of Charles II's Secretaries of State declared, was
"a sort of appeal to the people." In 1680 Chief Justice Scroggs
notified printers and booksellers that "to print or publish any
newsbooks or pamphlets of news whatsoever is illegal."

This meant that unorthodox points of view could no longer
be expressed. It may be that nobody continued to hold them,
but this seems unlikely. It also meant that those who wished
to publish had to trim their sails to the prevailing winds, and
to express themselves with caution. I noted earlier the tendency of radical political writers to draw their examples from
classical antiquity rather than from the history of the English
Revolution.[1] This refusal "to follow truth too near the

1. See p. 27 above.

heels"[2] was merely common prudence, but it has often deceived scholars into supposing that "the classical republicans" *derived* their ideas from the ancient world rather than from that in which they lived; just as Milton has been thought to derive from Greek philosophers or early Christian Fathers ideas which he could have met with in any London tavern in the sixteen-forties.[3]

All historians of seventeenth-century English literature should be made to read the letters of Chekhov, where they can see that great writer struggling against a very similar censorship. Sometimes he made concessions to the censor over what he regarded as less essential matters, in order to be able to make his main point; at other times he abandoned a story rather than emasculate it. Yet Chekhov was far from being a "political" writer. We should bear him in mind when thinking either of the much more political Milton, or of a writer like Bunyan whose works were thought by his superiors to have political implications. A licenser told Richard Baxter that censorship was exercised against an author's reputation as well as against a particular book. So though Milton put anti-Trinitarianism and defence of polygamy into *Paradise Lost,* he had to do it very carefully; he deceived many readers, especially after Addison had established his "respectable" reputation.

It seems to me that there is in effect a conspiracy between seventeenth-century censors and some twentieth-century literary critics who believe that a poem should speak for itself, divorced from history: who do not sufficiently consider the processes in consequence of which some words get on to the page and others get left off. One critic, for instance, argues in a simple syllogism, that Milton could have published an anti-Trinitarian poem; he did not: *ergo,* he was not an anti-

2. Sir Walter Raleigh, *History of the World,* 6 vols. (Edinburgh, 1820), I, lviii.
3. See my *Milton and the English Revolution* (London: Faber and Faber, 1977), *passim.*

Trinitarian. But the major premise is true only in the sense that Milton "could" have deliberately courted imprisonment or possibly death. Those who want to find "Christian humanism" in the writings of Shakespeare and his contemporaries can always find it; but it may be no more satisfactory as evidence of genuine beliefs than is Milton's "orthodoxy." It was what men were allowed to express. I recall Mr. Laslett's pious conviction (in *The World We Have Lost*) that in the seventeenth century "all of our ancestors were literal Christian believers, all the time." As soon as one looks seriously at the record one has doubts—or a very wide definition of "Christianity."

Because of the liberty of speech and publication which existed after 1640 we know more of what went before than of what happened after 1660. Many works were published in the forties and fifties which could not have appeared earlier because of "the iniquity of the times"—I quote from the title-page to the Puritan Thomas Taylor's posthumously published *Works* of 1653. Examples are Fulke Greville's *Life of Sidney,* the later volumes of Coke's *Institutes,* the memoirs of Sir Robert Naunton, Arthur Wilson, and Bishop Goodman, the millenarian writings of Joseph Mede, translations of Thomas Brightman, John Henry Alsted, and many others, William Gilbert's *Physiologia Nova,* many of Bacon's works, translations of William Harvey, etc. We happen to know that Sir Henry Spelman, Sir Simonds D'Ewes, and Joseph Mede deliberately refrained from publication before 1640: there must have been hundreds more. How many early seventeenth century poets and playwrights had their collected works published for the first time between 1640 and 1660?

Nor was the censorship effective in England only. When the great Puritan William Ames had gone into exile in the Netherlands he still could not escape the long arm of the English government. Through pressure on his patron and on the Dutch authorities he was persuaded, for a time at least, to drop attacks on the bishops in favour of attacks on papists and sectaries.[4] So we cannot assume that even in exile men were free to say what they really meant. When after Milton's death an attempt was made to publish his very heretical *De Doctrina Christiana* in the Netherlands, in Latin, the whole force of British diplomacy was mobilized to stop it. Not only was it not printed; the manuscript was seized and found its way into the State Paper Office, where it remained until 1823.

We cannot stress too strongly the uniqueness of the years 1640–60. The number of pamphlets published in England shot up from 22 in 1640 to 1966 in 1642—an increase of nearly 9000 percent once the press had been liberated from what Elias Ashmole called "the malice of the clergy." The number of newspapers, ballads, and almanacs increased in like proportion. The free printing of those years was colossally significant, not only because it provides us with historical source material. A printing press was a cheap piece of machinery. Broadsides were read in taverns even to the illiterate—and to the rank and file of the New Model Army. So all sorts of heresies were spread abroad —Socinianism, the Koran, free love, polygamy, divorce, the perfectibility of man. Above all, uncensored printing offered the possibility of choice between alternatives, ended the state church's monopoly of opinion-forming. Truth, as Milton said, might have more shapes than one. Even publications so apparently innocuous as almanacs contributed to radical politics. The Bodleian Library holds 24 different almanacs for the year 1654, some of them used by writers like Nicholas Culpeper and William Lilly for deliberate propaganda purposes.[5]

After 1660 a very determined attempt was made to suppress the memory of this freedom of speech and thought. We should

4. K. L. Sprunger, *The Learned Dr. William Ames: Dutch Backgrounds of English and American Puritanism* (Urbana: University of Illinois Press, 1972), pp. 33–35, 38.

5. This point has been elaborated by Capp, *Astrology and the Popular Press*, chaps. 3–5.

associate this with the frequently expressed hatred of grammar schools, which were blamed for the civil war, with the decline of literacy, and with eighteenth-century opposition to educating the poor. But there was much that could not be suppressed. Both John Aubrey and Sir William Temple date the end of belief in "fairies, sprites, witchcraft, and enchantments" to the revolutionary decades. The Marquis of Halifax thought that "the liberty of the late times gave men so much light, and diffused it so universally among the people, that they are not now to be dealt with as they might have been in an age of less inquiry."

I cannot do more than mention the effects of the pamphlets of the forties and fifties on prose styles. The object of the pamphleteers was to convince, to influence as many men as possible, often men of classes hitherto outside politics. They therefore cultivated a lively, conversational style, imitated the plain prose of the Puritan sermon. Their arguments had to be sensible and utilitarian. This was true not only of the explicitly propagandist pamphlets of Levellers, Diggers, Ranters, and Quakers, it was also true of the relatively novel genre of spiritual autobiography; and the new techniques were imitated by skilful royalist journalists like Sir John Berkenhead and by the versatile turncoat Marchamont Nedham. The rolling periods of Richard Hooker, Lancelot Andrewes, Sir Thomas Browne, even of John Milton's early pamphlets, were unsuitable for these rough-and-tumble purposes. The pamphleteers evolved a medium which looks forward both to restoration comedy and to Bunyan and Defoe. The Royal Society itself stressed the importance of clear, plain, straightforward, artisan's prose. It is difficult to assess the cumulative significance of this development on men's ways of thought as well as of expression. The age of revolution was also a great age of self-consciousness, of self-examination, of diaries as well as of spiritual autobiographies. Samuel Pepys started his Diary as an exercise in spiritual bookkeeping, though enjoyment would keep breaking in. All these tendencies point forward to the novel, catering for the newly leisured middle class, and especially its women.

One creation of the Revolution was a steady reading public, which may have been starved in the generation after 1660. But by the sixteen-nineties fear of radical revolution no longer applied. The Licensing Act lapsed in 1695, not in response to the principles of philosophical liberalism but in response to the pressure of profit-seeking printers and booksellers. By then writers were prepared to censor themselves: the market had created a new consensus. In 1759 Oliver Goldsmith wrote: "At present the few poets of England no longer depend on the Great for substance, they have now no other patrons but the public. . . . A writer of real merit now may easily be rich if his heart be set only on fortune." Men and women could earn a living as professional writers.

In art, merchant patronage succeeded that of the aristocracy. Sir Godfrey Kneller "owed his establishment in this country," Margaret Whinney and Oliver Millar tell us, "to the good offices of merchants, who were playing the parts which had been acted under the early Stuarts by [the Earl of] Arundel and the Duke of Buckingham." If we look forward to Hogarth, we can appreciate the extent of the revolution in taste since the days of Van Dyke. London's standards spread over the three kingdoms as the national market established itself. During the same period medical practice, Professor R. S. Roberts observed, became "a free economic activity like any other, its personnel and behaviour directed by the market." Apothecaries and other general practitioners escaped from the tutelage of the College of Physicians. Many doctors became very rich as this new professional class throve to gentility. But three out of four Englishmen, the Quaker social reformer John Bellers wrote in 1714, could not afford medical advice or treatment. The death rate among children of the poor was still horrific.

The three professions of divinity, law, medicine had been the target of radical attack during the Revolution. The radicals wanted to see a diffusion of do-it-yourself knowledge, and hated the specialization of the professions, which had to be paid for and therefore was more easily available to the rich than the poor. The rise in wealth and status of members of the learned professions and other town dwellers claiming to be gentlemen is another aspect of the evolution of a two-class society during and after the Revolution.[6]

6. Cf. A. Everitt, *Change in the Provinces: The Seventeenth Century* (Leicester University Press, 1969), pp. 43–46; cf. my *Change and Continuity in Seventeenth-Century England*, part III.

VIII

I TRIED EARLIER slightly to debunk the legend of monarchy. I should like to attempt the same for the legend of Puritans as black-clothed bigots, who went about whining psalms through their noses, desecrating churches, and killing joy. There were some such, but these were not the mainline Puritans of whom we should think when we are considering Puritanism as the ideology of the English Revolution. We should think rather of John Milton, lover of poetry and music, of Oliver Cromwell, lover of music and wine, of Major-General Harrison strutting about in his scarlet cloak, of Lucy Hutchinson who tells us that when her future husband came to court her he found "that though she was modest yet she was accostable" withal, and who remarked that Edward the Confessor was "sainted for his ungodly chastity." Quakers diverted converts from lacemaking to the less ungodly trade of brewing; Bunyan thought that a teetotaller lacked the spirit of God. It was Archbishop Laud who had the hair of Oxford undergraduates cut short; long hair luxuriated in the Oxford of the sixteen-fifties, when gowns were no longer worn.

The main enemies of the theatre were not Puritans, they were the City Fathers of London. Of the principal pamphleteers against the theatre, Philip Stubbe was a staunch defender of episcopacy, Stephen Gosson was an ex-actor who held a living in the Church of England, William Prynne was an Erastian lawyer, Jeremy Collier was a very high Anglican.[1] The charge

1. I owe these points to Miss Margot Heinemann.

of being killjoys may perhaps be laid at the door of some non-conformists at a much later date, after they had been excluded in 1660–62 from central and local government and from the universities. They were cut off from the great world of politics and from the styles of eloquence and political discourse which were fashionable in that world.

The social significance of the religious toleration established in the sixteen-forties had been that the lower orders could meet, discuss, and organize themselves, free from the control either of a parson safely educated at Oxford or Cambridge or of the squire, and free too from the paternal supervision of heads of families. The restoration of the episcopal church marked the defeat of this aspect of the radical revolution. A pamphlet of 1670, *A Private Conference between a Rich Alderman and a Poor Country Vicar,* reminded the gentry of the recent horrid times when *they* might have had to stand in a white sheet on the stool of repentance.

The sectarian congregations originated as something like underground revolutionary cells, surfacing in the sixteen-forties to discuss politics and economics as well as theology in the narrower sense. But after the Revolution's defeat, persecution weeded out all but the sincerest religious believers. As the looked-for millennium failed to arrive, men concluded that Christ's kingdom was not of this world. Fox led the Quakers into pacifism, abstention from politics, and sectarian exclusiveness. Other dissenters were *extruded* from the national church, forced to accept the status of sectaries, however reluctantly. After 1660 the old dissent was less concerned to convert their fellow-countrymen than to separate from them and survive. It was nearly another century before Wesley proclaimed that the world was his parish.

Ecclesiastical censorship came back in 1660: so did ecclesiastical control of education. The state church resumed its traditional role of monopoly opinion-forming, at least in the countryside, where the alliance of parson and squire was consolidated afresh. The ancien régime was restored in Oxford and Cambridge more completely than anywhere else. Scientists like Seth Ward and John Wilkins were ousted. Modern science, which had flourished in Oxford during the Revolution, now had to develop elsewhere, slowly: in the Royal Society of London, in the dissenting academies. Universities retained their monopoly of training clergymen for the state church. The political significance of this changed after 1689, when that church lost its total monopoly; but the universities were not reformed until the nineteenth century, and meanwhile dissenters remained excluded. The dissenting academies gave a better education than Oxford and Cambridge, but they lacked social cachet. In consequence religious divisions became social divisions. To be a dissenter was to be socially inferior. The nonconformist minority became, through no fault of its own, provincial, "sectarian" and "Puritan" in the pejorative sense of those words.

Looked at from this point of view the restoration was a social disaster, creating that two-class system in English educational life that has bedevilled it ever since—amateur rulers and M.P.s who can quote Horace on the one hand, a professional middle class and practical engineers on the other. And it led on to the sterile denominational controversies over education in the nineteenth century. After 1660 there was even less of an educational ladder than before 1640: the talents of the lower classes were not drawn on for the Industrial Revolution.[2] The principle of the steam engine was known for a very long time before it was applied. A few lower-class men of genius made their way to the top, but there was no educational reform, as there was no political or legal reform, till the nineteenth century. Things might have been different if some of the educa-

2. C. Webster, "Science and the Challenge to the Scholastic Curriculum, 1640–1660," in *The Changing Curriculum* (History of Education Society, 1971), pp. 32–34.

tional projects to which the Revolution gave birth had been carried through, and a mobile society of the career open to the talents established. The failure was long concealed by the flying start which the British economy received; but the insecurity of its educational base has been revealed in the present century—revealed but not yet adequately reformed.

Only in towns could dissent not be eliminated. Conventicles, it was claimed in 1675, can be suppressed "in the country where the gentry live and the people have a dependence on them, . . . but in corporations it will never be carried through by the magistrates or the inhabitants, their livelihood consisting altogether in trade, and their depending one upon another, so that when any of them shall appear to act in the least measure, their trade shall decline and . . . their credit with it."[3] There was some consumers' choice in religion in the towns.

The episcopal Church of England was restored as the army of the propertied. "If there was not a minister in every parish," said Robert South, former eulogist of Cromwell, "you would quickly find cause to increase the number of constables."[4] But the church restored in 1660 was not the Laudian church. There was no High Commission to give teeth to the censures of church courts, and none of the other prerogative courts was restored. "Churchwardens' presentments are but laughed at," we hear from Lancashire in 1669. Excommunication was "only their not going to church," men who refused to pay tithe on wages told one another in 1683.[5] Bishops no longer held significant state office. The will of government and bishops could

3. *Calendar of State Papers, Domestic, 1675–76* (HMSO, London, 1907), p. 1. For neighbours and even constables protecting Quakers, see, for example, Daniel Roberts, *Some Memoirs of the Life of John Roberts, 1623–83* (1973 reprint), pp. 54, 73, 75, 79, 82, 91, and *passim*.

4. Quoted in Irène Simon, ed., *Three Restoration Divines: Barrow, South, Tillotson* (Bibliothèque de la Faculté de Philosophie et Lettres de l'Université de Liège, Fascicule 181, 1967–76), II, 60; cf. I, 240.

5. B. Nightingale, *Early Stages of the Quaker Movement in Lancashire* (London:

not be imposed when it conflicted with the will of those whom the House of Commons represented, or with the common-law courts. The end of separate taxation of the clergy led to the end of Convocation as a serious representative body. The Laudian attempt to elevate the social and political status of the clergy was totally defeated. The cessation of the generous augmentations which had been established in some parishes during the Revolution reduced parsons there to even greater dependence on the squires—and by 1680 there was a resident squire in three villages out of four. As recipients of tithes in kind most of the clergy benefited from the agricultural boom of the late-seventeenth and eighteenth centuries, but by then they were politically tied to the coat-tails of the gentry, no longer the leaders of opinion which they had aspired to be in the early and mid seventeenth century.

I have mentioned millenarianism from time to time, the realization of Christ's kingdom on earth. For decades men of the first intellectual capacity applied themselves to study of the biblical prophecies—John Napier, Thomas Brightman, Joseph Mede, later Newton. By 1640 there had come to be a consensus that great events were likely to happen in the sixteen-fifties and nineties. During the civil war Parliamentarian preachers announced Jesus Christ as shortly expected King, and called on the humble and lowly to fight in order to bring his reign about. This line of thought derived from John Foxe's immensely popular *Book of Martyrs*, in which the common people of England were shown as being always in the forefront of the fight against Antichrist, whilst their social betters lagged behind.

But when the war ended, and the kingdom of God did not appear, when on the contrary God's servants were bitterly divided on major political issues, and the peace was kept only by

---

Congregational Union of England and Wales, 1921), p. 72; my *Economic Problems of the Church,* Panther edition, p. 86.

an army which cost exorbitant sums in taxation and free quarter, then the millenarian dream faded. The crucial dates of the fifties passed: instead of King Jesus, the Merrie Monarch occupied the throne. Hope deferred made the heart sick. Men had to rethink, either the chronology, or the whole concept of a divine kingdom on earth. "Take heed of computing," wrote the Independent John Owen in 1680. "How woefully and wretchedly have we been mistaken by this." Sir Isaac Newton still went on secretly trying to solve the chronological problems of the Second Coming; but it receded further and further into the future, ceased to be practical politics. In 1694 John Mason announced that the end of the world was at hand, and that only those at Water Stratford would survive; large crowds collected there, but he was not rushed off to prison, as he would have been a generation earlier. He was advised to take physic.

Yet millenarianism left its mark on ways of thinking about this world. "We look for a new earth as well as a new heaven," wrote the Quaker leader Edward Burrough in October 1659. After the restoration John Dryden in *Annus Mirabilis* converted millenarianism to the uses of a monarchy which he believed would make England mistress of the trade of the world. Thomas Sprat had a similar vision in *The History of the Royal Society of London,* and Sir Peter Pett wrote: "one kind of a new heaven and a new earth that perhaps we may shortly see in old England" would come "when the necessary improvement of our land by our numerous people shall have enriched as many as deserve to be so, and when . . . the effects of diligence fill all hands with profit and eyes with pleasure."[6]

Historians of literature have perhaps taken too much for granted the emergence of new assumptions about the role of economics in English life, deriving from the Navigation Act

6. Quoted by J. R. Jacob, *Robert Boyle and the English Revolution* (New York: B. Franklin, 1977), p. 158.

and the expansionist foreign policy which Cromwell initiated. When Dryden set the idyllic scene for his dialogue between court wits, published as *An Essay of Dramatic Poesy* in 1668, he tells us that it took place during the second Dutch War, on "that memorable day . . . wherein the two most mighty and best appointed fleets which any age had ever seen disputed the command of the greater half of the globe, the commerce of nations, and the riches of the universe." It would have been totally impossible for an aspiring young man of letters to have written in such terms before 1640. England then had no such economic power, and courtiers had no such economic interests. Yet now it was respectable and indeed patriotic to accept the fact that England's interests (including the interests of the aristocracy) were inextricably bound up with an aggressive commercial imperialism. Economics has replaced religion, economic nationalism millenarian internationalism. We can regard this as more realistic or coarser according to taste. The concerns of court wits (and the Royal Society) under Charles II are at least less trivial than those of Charles I's courtiers, even if they are more openly and brutally materialistic than those of the public figures of the Commonwealth and Protectorate.

In the long run perhaps this is the most interesting legacy of the millenarianism of the Revolution—the hopes it raised for a *new* utopian future on earth. Initially all the revolutionaries had looked to the past—Levellers for a recovery of Anglo-Saxon freedom, sectaries for a return to primitive Christianity, Diggers and Quakers for a recapture of Adam's state of innocence and power before the Fall. Millenarianism shifted the golden age to the future. Once it had shaken off its apocalyptic associations, it could easily link up with Bacon's scientific optimism to form a theory of progress. Dryden after all was a Fellow of the Royal Society. Robert Hooke's Preface to his treatise on the microscope suggested that "as at first mankind fell by tasting the forbidden tree of knowledge, so we their posterity may be in part restored . . . by tasting . . . those fruits of natural knowledge that were never yet forbidden." So we look forward to the eighteenth-century doctrine of *secular* progress.

Calvinism had assumed that all mankind must suffer for Adam's sin at the beginning of history, and that there was nothing that any individual could do to avert or mitigate his fate. Sir Robert Filmer assumed in his *Patriarcha* that the absolute rule of kings derived from the rights of Adam over all his children. In *Absalom and Achitophel* Dryden noted the connection between the doctrines of original sin and passive obedience to monarchical authority. Both assume that posterity is inexorably bound by actions taken by distant ancestors. By the end of the seventeenth century Calvinism has lost its intellectual dominance, and Locke has routed Filmer (though it is significant that he still thought him worth refuting). This too contributed to a shift in political thinking, from the past to the future, from the hereditary principle which had dominated in a relatively static agrarian society to the atomic individualism and contractualism more appropriate to a mobile and expansive economy.

The end of millenarianism coincided with the rise of pacifism among the sects, notably the Quakers, who in the fifties had been both more millenarian and more political than used to be thought. The panic of 1659–60—and it was a panic—was directed against "fanatics," against enthusiasm. General Lambert was thought to be arming the Quakers—not as unlikely as it seems to those of us who have got used to the pacifism which the Quakers adopted after 1660. One of the conscious aims of the Royal Society was to combat "fanaticism," "enthusiasm." In a valuable series of articles Professor J. R. Jacob has shown how deeply this attitude permeated the thinking of Robert Boyle, from at least the sixteen-fifties, when he and his circle had seen Cromwell as God's agent for the destruction of Antichrist. Before and after the restoration a principal aim of

Boyle's philosophy was "to steal the sectaries' . . . thunder," to reject mortalism and deism; at the same time that his brother, Lord Broghill, was first Cromwell's right-hand man in shifting the government of the Protectorate in a conservative direction, then an active supporter of the restoration of Charles II and the pioneer of "heroic drama" after the French fashion, in rhymed couplets. Boyle continued to attack enthusiasm and the sectaries after the restoration, and the Royal Society took up the same struggle.[7]

7. J. R. Jacob, "The Ideological Origins of Robert Boyle's Natural Philosophy," *Journal of European Studies* 2 (1971): 1–21, esp. 15, 18, 21; "Robert Boyle and Subversive Religion in the Early Restoration," *Albion* 6 (1974): 275–93; "Boyle's Circle in the Protectorate: Revelation, Politics and the Millennium," *Journal of the History of Ideas* 38 (1977): 131–40. Cf. the argument of M. McKeon's *Politics and Poetry in Restoration England: The Case of Dryden's Annus Mirabilis* (Harvard University Press, 1975), esp. the Conclusion; and Lindsay Sharp, "Timber, Science and Economic Reform in the Seventeenth Century," *Forestry* (1975): 61, 67–68, 78. For heroic drama see p. 25 above.

IX

THERE HAS BEEN a lot of controversy among historians about the origins of the Royal Society, a controversy which got bogged down in rival statistical exercises. After defining "Puritan" or "Parliamentarian" in a way that suited your argument (or not defining terms at all) you then counted Fellows of the Royal Society and concluded: "There now: they all were (or were not) Puritans." One such counter assumed that no one who became a bishop after 1660 could have been a Puritan; another employed a definition of "Puritan" which would have excluded men like Baxter and Milton. Professor Jacob's approach, through ideology rather than personality, shows the Royal Society to have been composed mainly of those who later came to be known as "Latitudinarians," the word used to describe ex-Puritans who conformed to the restored episcopal church in 1660, or other conformists who had accepted the Cromwellian state church. Their "Puritanism" was of the main-line type which goes back to William Perkins, John Preston, and Richard Sibbes. Since the late sixteenth century such Puritans had seen themselves as conducting a struggle on two fronts—against popery and against radical sectarianism. It was therefore natural after 1660 for the Latitudinarians to denounce "enthusiasm," "fanaticism," the radicalism of the extremer sects. The classical exposition of their position was the propagandist *History of the Royal Society*, written by Thomas Sprat, former eulogist of Oliver Cromwell and later bishop. The Secretary of the Royal Society was John Wilkins, author of a treatise on Puritan preaching, brother-in-law of Oliver Cromwell, and later Bishop of Chester.

In a striking book complementary to the work of J. R. Jacob, Margaret Jacob has argued that the Latitudinarians "devised a natural religion comprehensive enough to override doctrinal differences and so broad in its application as to include behaviour once labelled simply as antichristian." "The most historically significant contribution of the latitudinarians lies in their ability to synthesize the operations of a market society and the workings of nature in such a way as to render the market society natural." "The latitudinarians were trying to stem a tide, not to hold back the growth of capitalistic forms of economic and social life, but to Christianize them." They wanted to tame Hobbes's social philosophy as Locke tamed his political philosophy.[1]

She extends this from the organization to the content of science. "The new mechanical philosophy triumphed in England" not "simply because it offered the most plausible explanation of nature" but because "the ordered, providentially guided, mathematically regulated universe of Newton gave a model for a stable and prosperous polity, ruled by the self-interest of men," escaping from the materialistic atheism, the encouragement of rapacious self-interest and the political absolutism implicit in Hobbism. Science was attacked in the sixties because of its supposed atheistic tendencies and because of the scientists' acceptance of the revolutionary régimes: it took a lot of propaganda like Sprat's before science became respectable.[2]

This makes much better sense of science during the restoration period, and of the Royal Society, than any explanation derived from counting Fellows. The scientists who gathered in London in 1660 took great pains to win the patronage of Charles II, and to recruit as many courtiers and budding bishops as they could. Any peer who condescended to join their

1. Margaret C. Jacob, *The Newtonians and the English Revolution, 1689–1720* (Ithaca, Cornell University Press, and Hassocks, Harvester Press, 1976), pp. 49–51, 68.
2. Ibid., pp. 17–18, 38–39, 53.

gentleman's club was gratefully accepted. This helps to explain the vulgar utilitarian emphasis, especially on agricultural improvements, as well as the gadgetry which looms so large in the Society's early experiments, designed to entertain the Fellows. Hence the exclusion of the "atheist" Hobbes and the radical Hartlib. Hence the rapid decline of English science, except in abstract mathematics, hence the inability of the Royal Society to contribute to the thinking which underlay the innovations of the Industrial Revolution.

The seventeenth century saw a general decline of magic. In 1600 most respectable opinion believed in witches and "touching" for the King's Evil; by 1700 this was no longer true. An important contribution to this growing rationalism was the free discussion of the forties and fifties. But the old ideas died hard. In the early seventeenth century the lines were not drawn clearly. Astrologers and alchemists still made real contributions to science: Boyle and Newton continued to study alchemy, Locke believed in sympathetic magic. But in the second half of the century the mechanical philosophy gradually replaced animism, magic. There was a Puritan contribution to this—rational critique of the miracle of the mass, of holy water, exorcism, etc., rejection of mediating saints and the Virgin, an emphasis on the study of God's works in nature. During a transitional stage this led to an increase in men's belief in the power of the devil, to greater authority for the cunning man or white witch.[3] Calvinism can from this point of view be seen as the religion of the *haute bourgeoisie* as against the more magical beliefs of the radical sects.[4] The latitudinarianism of many members of the Royal Society was the culmination, in different circumstances, of this trend: enthusiasm was rejected in science as in religion or politics.

In explaining the decline of magic Mr. K. V. Thomas empha-

3. K. V. Thomas, *Religion and the Decline of Magic* (London, Weidenfeld and Nicolson, and New York, Scribner, 1971), chap. 15.
4. See my *The World Turned Upside Down*, chap. 14.

sizes increasing human control over the environment, better communications, fire-fighting devices, technical improvements in agriculture and industry, the concept of statistical probability.[5] We may add the greater political stability of the post-revolutionary period, reduction of arbitrariness (at least for the propertied classes), the common law's victory over the prerogative, the end of plague, national prosperity. The successful political activities of Parliament and people during the Revolution led to a greater belief in the possibilities of human action to control nature, linking up with the discovery of the New World and the new heavens, the use of astronomy for navigation. There was more widespread medical knowledge, thanks in large part to the translations and treatises which could be published during the Revolution and which helped to reduce reliance on "cunning men."

But the mechanical philosophy brought with it the end of the universe as a comprehensible whole. Knowledge was no longer shut up from the common people in Latin, but in the technical vocabulary of the specialized sciences. The revolutionary decades saw the last attempts at an overall synthesis of knowledge—the wide social vision of the Baconians and the Comenian reformers recently studied by Charles Webster[6]; the communist world-view of Gerrard Winstanley, the great synthesis of *Paradise Lost.* As these faded we get a departmentalization of specialized sciences, including the sciences of politics and economics, now separated from theology as Bacon had separated natural science from theology. Division of labour in the arts intensified professionalism. As we have seen, the development of the market led to the emergence of new professions—writers, architects, virtuoso concert performers, painters, actresses.[7]

5. Thomas, *Religion*, chap. 22.
6. C. Webster, *The Great Instauration: Science, Medicine and Reform, 1626–1660* (London: Duckworth, 1975).
7. See pp. 51–52 above.

So an abstract mechanism came to replace the animism of the old cosy magical universe. Direct correspondence between the cosmos and man could no longer be observed. Angels ceased to push the planets around, wounds ceased to be cured by applying medicine to the weapon which caused them; intellectuals ceased to believe that important actions should be performed at the best conjunction of the planets if they were to be effective; the music of the spheres ceased, and was replaced by the eternal silence of infinite space which so terrified Pascal. Cosmic equality under the sun, whether the units were planets, men, or atoms, replaced the traditional hierarchy of the great chain of being. Man found himself alone in an unfriendly universe. God and the devil no longer took an active, day-to-day interest in humanity. Magic slowly died with the village community from which it had drawn its strength; so did the songs and dances of the peasantry. The last witch was burnt in England in 1685. Newton never published his alchemical researches: the Newtonians proclaimed God the great watchmaker. Constitutional law ruled in heaven no less than on earth.

The political revulsion against "fanaticism," "enthusiasm," radicalism, thus helped to produce a new rational religion which tended towards deism. Halifax saw God Almighty as a Trimmer, suspended between his mercy and his justice. Locke and many others stressed *The Reasonableness of Christianity*, Toland argued for a *Christianity Not Mysterious*. The God of Milton, Bunyan, and Oliver Cromwell had been rather different. The temperature was lowered. By the eighteenth century Presbyterian congregations, under pressure from their lay members, were moving towards Unitarianism. Similarly Locke by treating the state as a limited liability company, ringholder in the free-for-all of capitalism, accepted the Hobbist transformation of politics into a rational science, in which texts and precedents, divine hereditary right, lost their point; but avoided Hobbes's extremer intellectual and political conclusions. Rea-

66

son and utility were now more important than emotion, just as property was more important than life. This emphasis on empiricism, common sense, was admirable in many ways, but it worked to the special advantage of a limited class. England after 1688 was the freest country in the world if you had money. But it contrasted with Winstanley's vision of a united and equal community, in which labour and knowledge would be pooled in order to make a more beautiful commonwealth; with the Leveller vision of a self-governing democracy, in which there would be no lawyers; with the educational reformers' schemes for free education for both sexes, all classes, and all ages; and indeed with Milton's vision of Christ as the "shortly-expected King" who would put an end to "all earthly tyrannies." There was loss as well as gain in the undoubted social progress that was registered between 1600 and 1700.

X

THE RADICAL Puritan revolution was defeated; but after 1660 the Latitudinarians outweighted the former Laudians, who had remained aloof from the Cromwellian establishment and bitterly resented the dominance of men who had cheerfully accepted a non-episcopal church. As we saw, many aspects of Laudianism could not be resurrected. In this business-like world Puritan plain preaching made the conceited scholarly style of Lancelot Andrewes and the Caroline court divines sound old-fashioned. Lectureships, originating in Puritan protest, were absorbed into the post-restoration establishment.[1] The elevation of preaching above the sacraments even affected ecclesiastical architecture.[2] Charles II showed his usual acumen, and his usual disregard for truth, when on his arrival at Dover in May 1660 he told the mayor who presented him with a Bible that he valued it above all things. Dryden in *Absalom and Achitophel* used biblical imagery for contemporary political purposes no less successfully than Milton and the Puritan preachers. Sabbatarianism, formerly the hall-mark of Puritanism, was accepted by the Church of England after 1660, the rhythms of an agricultural society yielding place to those more appropriate to an industrial society.[3] "The profanation of the Lord's day by open sports and pastimes is by the civil part of the nation ac-

1. See my *Society and Puritanism in Pre-Revolutionary England,* Panther edition (1969), chaps. 2 and 3, for an elaboration of this point.
2. See p. 79 below.
3. *Society and Puritanism,* chap. 5.

counted scandalous," wrote John Corbet in 1660; and by now kings and bishops had to follow "the civil part of the nation": things had been different when James and Charles I issued their Books of Sports licensing such pastimes on Sundays. After some prodding by the House of Commons, Charles II's Worcester House Declaration of October 1660 promised "to take care that the Lord's day be applied to holy exercises, without unnecessary divertisements." In 1662, again in response to a request from Parliament, the King wrote to the Archbishop of Canterbury to urge "better observing of the Lord's Day, much neglected of late." In 1663, at the request of the Commons, he issued a proclamation against Sunday travelling. Finally the 1677 Sabbath Act summed up the legislation of the revolutionary epoch which proscribed Sunday work.

Church courts revived briefly in the sixties and seventies and were used in the struggle against nonconformity. J. P.s gradually took over the courts' traditional task of moral supervision, which became increasingly a matter of protecting rate-payers from the expense of maintaining bastards. By the end of the century ecclesiastical discipline had waned to such an extent that voluntary Societies for the Reformation of Manners were formed, containing nonconformists as well as Anglicans, to enforce morality on the lower orders.

The Latitudinarians, Mrs. Jacob tells us, "were neither more nor less keen on promoting industry and trade than were the non-conforming preachers." One of them, Tillotson, proclaimed that "virtue promotes our outward temporal interests." "This is the wisdom of religion, that . . . it does advise and lead us to our best interest." Even knaves ought to be virtuous, "with a crafty design to promote and advance more effectually their own interests." As Professor Schlatter put it, "the Puritan instructed Christians to serve God by being good men of business; the Anglican instructed business men to serve themselves by being godly."[4] Locke's philosophy was a secularized Puritanism.

The Revolution did however secure positive gains in the religious sphere. Discipline by the purse, so bitterly attacked by Milton, came to an end. (But Milton no less than Locke assumed that conscience would accept the sanctity of the property "even of wicked men.") The decay of church courts, and the failure to establish an alternative Presbyterian discipline, meant that sin was permanently distinguished from crime, became a private not a public concern. All those above the social level of the poor subject to the supervision of J.P.s henceforth took their own moral decisions. There is a great intellectual and moral revolution in the replacement of church courts by conscience; correct observance of external forms and ceremonies became less important than the intention behind an action; virtue is to be pursued for its own sake, not for fear of punishment, even in the next world. "If there were no God to reward the good nor punish the evil," Lodowick Muggleton declared, "yet could I not do other ways than I do; for I do well, not because I expect any reward from God, and I refrain from evil, not for fear God should see me, or seeing me will punish me; . . . but I do well, and refrain from evil, to please the law written in my heart, so that I might not be accused in my own conscience." At the same time belief in a local geographical hell had come under attack, both from the radical theologians of the revolutionary sects and from problems posed by the new astronomy.[5]

We find, then, a convergence of theological trends against

4. M. C. Jacob, *The Newtonians,* chap. 1, *passim;* J. Tillotson, *Sermons on Several Subjects and Occasions* (London: 1748), IX, 134–36; R. B. Schlatter, *The Social Ideas of Religious Leaders, 1660–1688* (London: Oxford University Press, 1940), p. 203.

5. L. Muggleton, *The Acts of the Witnesses of the Spirit* (London, 1764), p. 140 (first published 1699); D. P. Walker, *The Decline of Hell: Discussions of Eternal Torment in the Seventeenth Century* (University of Chicago Press, 1964), *passim.*

Calvinism. Before 1640 the Calvinist theology, with its concept of the oligarchy of the predestined elect, its emphasis on discipline, was attacked from the right by sacramentalist Laudian Arminians; during the Revolution it was attacked by rationalist Arminians of the left—John Goodwin, Milton, Quakers. The Presbyterian discipline was unpopular both with the ungodly lower classes and with upper-class anti-clericals. More serious, Calvinism proved unable to maintain its defences against antinomianism, the belief that the elect were above the moral law. So long as those who thought themselves the elect were respectable bourgeois Puritans, their sense of freedom through co-operation with God brought no fundamental danger to the social order. But it proved impossible, once discipline broke down, to decide who the elect were. God said very different things to lower-class consciences. Mechanic preachers and lower-class Quakers were convinced that the holy spirit was within them. Artisan Fifth Monarchists proclaimed that they were the saints who should rule. Some Ranters preached a dionysiac antinomianism that would have subverted all the moral standards of a propertied society. The radicals rejected as hypocrites those Puritans whose faith did not result in works of love.

Failure to agree on who were the elect drove the men of property back to a theology of works—by their fruits ye shall know them. Standards and norms of conduct could be established by lay J.P.s, with no danger of a clerical discipline. This was a very different theology of works from that of Catholics or Laudians; it was non-sacramental, in no way dependent on a mediating priesthood. It avoided both Laudian and Presbyterian clericalism. The sects themselves, once they had abandoned hope of Christ's kingdom here and now and had accepted the sinfulness of man, co-operated in enforcing a morality of works on their members. We are all so much Arminians now that it requires a great imaginative effort to think ourselves back into the pre-revolutionary society which Calvinism dominated. It was yet another route by which traditional Christian orthodoxy passed into deism: morals, conduct, became more important than theology.

Calvinism, like Roman Catholicism, was an international religion. Laud, who severed England's connections with French and Dutch Calvinists, had been a little Englander, provincial in outlook. But the Calvinist international effectively ceased to exist during the Thirty Years War, when France (with the support of Charles I) suppressed her Huguenot rebels before intervening on the "protestant" side. Cromwell's alliance with France against Spain continued this policy. Yet though no crusade to liberate Europe from popery emerged from the English Revolution (some Englishmen no doubt regarded the conquest of Ireland in that light!), anti-popery still remained powerful. It was reinforced and linked with hostility to absolutism in the later seventeenth century by fear of the France of Louis XIV. Daniel Defoe, looking back from the beginning of the eighteenth century, remarked of the early sixteen-seventies, "how many honest but over-frighted people set to work to copy the Bible into shorthand, lest when popery came in we should be prohibited the use of it. . . . At which work I myself, then but a boy, worked like a horse till I wrote out the whole Pentateuch, and then was so tired that I was willing to run the risk of the rest." Defoe was the son of a Presbyterian tallow-chandler. Higher in the social scale John Aubrey, also in the sixteen-seventies, was thinking of becoming a parson. "But," he noted, "the King of France grows stronger and stronger, and what if the Roman religion should come in again?" If he had "a good parsonage of £2 or £300 *per annum*" the bachelor Aubrey admitted, this "would be a shrewd temptation."[6]

6. M. Shinagel, *Defoe and Middle-Class Gentility* (Harvard University Press, 1968), p. 7; Anthony Powell, *John Aubrey and His Friends* (London, 1963), pp. 148, 167.

Cromwell's attempt in the fifties to unite all protestants in a single state church, with toleration outside, was the culmination of a century of Puritan endeavour: its failure marks the end of the protestant oecumenicism for which John Dury and others had laboured so constantly. Henceforth there were in England two protestant nations as well as the Roman Catholic minority. Again this perhaps goes back to Laud, or even earlier: his type of single all-embracing state church had become impossible well before the Revolution. The only question remaining was whether there should be a pluralist arrangement within a comprehensive national church, or outside it (toleration, sects, and occasional conformity).

Cromwell's church had aimed at incorporating radical protestants and excluding to the right; the Church of England after 1660 incorporated to the right and excluded the radicals. The sects had organized themselves on a national scale in the liberty of the forties and fifties. There was a Baptist confession in 1644; the Congregationalists followed suit in 1658. But Baptist and Congregationalist ministers held livings in the Cromwellian church. The Quakers were the first nationally organized sect which rejected any compromise with a state church; their example may have helped to harden Baptist attitudes. By the end of the fifties Quakers, Muggletonians, General and Particular Baptists, were organized on a sectarian basis. After 1662 they were joined, at first very reluctantly, by Presbyterians and Congregationalists, deliberately excluded from the episcopal Church of England.

In 1662 the Presbyterian Philip Henry was "loath . . . to encourage the people to separate," even though he himself felt constrained to resign his living rather than conform. Lay members of Presbyterian congregations seem to have had fewer inhibitions about accepting sectarian status. When in 1672 Charles II issued his Declaration of Indulgence Henry wrote that "the danger is lest the allowance of separate places [of worship] help to overthrow our parish-order . . . and beget divisions and animosities amongst us which no honest heart but would rather should be healed." He faced a "trilemma"—"either to turn flat Independents, or to strike in with the conformists, or to sit down in former silence and suffering till the Lord shall open a more effectual door." The Independents—i.e., the separating Congregationalists—in Henry's view "unchurch the nation; they pluck up the hedge of parish order." It was only logical for such a man to be an occasional conformist.

In the same year 1672 the Independent John Owen spoke of those "who separate, or rather are driven, from the present public worship." Four years later he claimed that such men "do sacredly adhere unto . . . the doctrine of the Church of England . . . as it is contained in the Articles of Religion, the Books of Homilies, and declared in the authenticated writings of all the learned prelates and others for sixty years after the Reformation." Dissenters, he was claiming, were the true Church of England. The high-flying Henry Sacheverell, on the other hand, in 1709 denounced "that false son of the church, Bishop Grindal," Elizabeth's Archbishop of Canterbury. Occasional conformity then, the means by which dissenters might qualify for office in local government, was not necessarily hypocritical. But nonconformists were liable to be accused of plotting, however much they rejected political solutions in favour of other-worldly ones. Elias Ashmole told his brother-in-law Henry Newcome in 1664 that "nonconformity could be nothing but in expectation of a change."[7]

7. *Autobiography of Henry Newcome,* ed. R. Parkinson (Chetham Society, vol. XXVI, 1852), I, 145.

XI

IN SOCIOLOGICAL TERMS the Presbyterian discipline had offered a means of imposing new mores, of enforcing the protestant ethic, a stricter monogamous morality, labour discipline, sabbath observance against the traditional rural festivals. Presbyterianism was overthrown by the New Model Army, and was equally disliked by conservatives. But some such discipline was socially necessary as England became a modern industrial nation. Ironically, the defeated sects took over the task of disciplining their own members, far more effectively than Anglican church courts or Presbyterian classes could have done. Baptists for instance used the distribution of poor relief as an instrument of social control. It was a sin, the Fenstanton Baptists decided, to keep a daughter at home in idleness, when she could earn her living in domestic service. Idleness and failure to pay debts were "great evils," especially when a member of the congregation was arrested, "to the dishonour of God."[1] In 1672 strong opposition was expressed among Richard Haines's fellow Baptists to his monopoly patent for making stronger cider. The objection was not on teetotal grounds. The church classed patentees with idolators and unclean persons: they were of bad repute in the world and a cause of offence to weaker brethren. They were threatened with excommunication. Quakers were as severe as Baptists against extravagance and indebtedness.[2]

1. *Records of the Churches of Christ Gathered at Fenstanton, Warboys and Hexham*, ed. E. B. Underhill (Hanserd Knollys Society, 1854), pp. 210, 229; cf. pp. 16–19, 85, 234.
2. C. R. Haines, *A Complete Memoir of Richard Haines, 1633–1685*, 2 vols.

The sects ceased to proselytize among the urban poor: it was all they could do to look after their own. They became increasingly anxious not to frighten off those of their members who began to prosper.

What we say about the church as a monopoly opinion-forming body in the seventeenth century must always be qualified by the fact that some sections of the population managed altogether to escape from its ministrations. Only we do not know how many. After 1660 the *de facto* existence of sects meant that in towns there was no effective enforcement of church attendance. But even before 1640 the church's claim to be all-embracing was not justified. Rogues and vagabonds, masterless men and beggars, almost certainly did not normally attend. Thus Donne asked, "How few of these who make beggary an occupation from their infancy were ever within church, how few of them ever christened, or ever married?" Wallace Notestein suggested that farm labourers and the very poor probably did not attend; the sectaries in the revolutionary decades may have been the first to appeal to them—yet another reason for the restoration.

In 1650 compulsory attendance at one's parish church was altogether abolished. Though it was restored in 1657, there is ample evidence that the situation was never recovered even after 1660. Matthew Robinson in his Richmondshire parish tells us that "many poor people . . . rarely attended the public worship on the Lord's days"; parish relief had to be withheld to compel them. In 1669 the churchwardens of a Hertfordshire parish thought it worth reporting that "several of the inhabitants come constantly to church." In 1680 in Kent "many of the meaner sort . . . absent themselves": this was said to be "the general complaint of all the parishes." In 1699 one Wor-

---

(London: Harrison and Sons, 1899), pp. 37–52; A. Lloyd, *Quaker Social History, 1669–1738* (London: Longmans, Green, 1950), pp. 2, 9, 37, 71–72; cf. Bunyan, *Works,* ed. G. Offor, 3 vols. (Glasgow, Edinburgh, and London, 1860), II, 582–83.

cestershire parson had no congregation at all.[3] Church courts had effectively ceased to function before the Toleration Act of 1689 completed the rout. We are back in the situation which prevailed between the 1650 act abolishing compulsory church attendance and 1657.

There is no space to consider in detail the long-term influence of those doctrinal heresies which were widely preached during the freedom of the Revolution. There were several varieties of anti-Trinitarianism, including those of Winstanley, Milton, Muggleton, Locke, and Newton. The most radical was Socinianism, which virtually denied the divinity of Christ and employed wholly rationalist arguments. The humanizing of the Son was accompanied by kicking the Father upstairs to become Law with a capital L: another route to deism. Eighteenth-century Unitarianism, tamed of the "enthusiastic" "excesses" of radical Socinianism, was accepted by many old dissenters.

The mortalist heresy—shared by Winstanley and Milton with Richard Overton the Leveller and the Muggletonians—gave religious faith a very this-worldly emphasis. The belief that souls slept or remained dead until the general resurrection finally refuted the idea of Purgatory, and so by implication rejected ghosts, spirits, witches—the supernatural generally. Fellows of the Royal Society came to the rescue of the irrational: Henry More, Joseph Glanvill, and Sir Thomas Browne felt that in defending the existence of spirits and witches they were defending the existence of God. An extreme group of mortalists, including Clarkson and probably Winstanley, rejected any final resurrection of the dead. So both the consolations of immortality and hell the great deterrent disappeared. This con-

3. *The Autobiography of Matthew Robinson,* ed. J. E. B. Mayor (1856), p. 61; B. S. Capp, *The Fifth Monarchy Men: A Study in Seventeenth-Century Millenarianism* (Totowa, N.J.: Rowman & Littlefield, 1972), p. 195; C. W. Chalkin, *Seventeenth-Century Kent: A Social and Economic History* (New York: Fernhill, 1965), p. 224; Geoffrey Holmes, *The Trial of Dr. Sacheverell* (London: Eyre Methuen, 1973), p. 25.

tributed to that evolution of a more disinterested morality which we have already considered.[4] Here too we are far along the road towards secularization.

During the Revolution antinomians like Abiezer Coppe and Lawrence Clarkson proclaimed that sin was abolished, or had never existed and was (like hell) a bugbear invented by the ruling class to terrorize their inferiors. Henry Denne, Joseph Bauthumley, Richard Coppin, as well as James Nayler, George Fox, and other Quakers, denounced preachers who "roar up for sin in their pulpits." Many believed with Milton, Ranters, and early Quakers that it was possible to get back in this world to a state of perfection superior to that enjoyed by Adam and Eve before the Fall. Winstanley taught that man fell when private property was established; the replacement of private property and wage labour by communual ownership and production would undo the consequences of the Fall. All "the inward bondages of the mind" would disappear when "the outward bondage that one sort of people lay upon another" was removed. The defeat of the Revolution destroyed this optimistic hope. As Christ's kingdom receded from this world to the next, Clarkson turned Muggletonian, sin reappeared in Quaker theology, sin looms larger in *Paradise Lost* than in *Areopagitica*. The clergy restored in 1660 did not fail to ram the point home. "Nothing else can so effectively enslave the common people," wrote a future bishop approvingly, "as the fear of invisible power and the dismal apprehensions of the world to come."

But it was not only a matter of pressure from above: the deism and rationalism of many intellectuals in the late seventeenth and early eighteenth centuries co-existed with a renewed emphasis in popular preaching on the sinfulness of the mass of humanity, which extends from Bunyan to Wesley, Whitfield, and Jabez Bunting. (The latter, it will be recalled, said that

4. See pp. 70 above and 80–81 below.

Methodism was opposed to democracy because it was opposed to sin—an argument which had been used against the seventeenth-century radicals.) Whether one adopted the bland optimistic religion of benevolence, or that of the hell-fire preachers, was in part a matter of temperament; but there are also social distinctions to be drawn. Calvinism descended the social scale at a time when many members of the middle and professional classes were escaping from helpless subordination to the blind forces of nature and the market. An arbitrary and capricious deity still seemed to make sense to the lower classes, trembling on the poverty line; and many of their betters were content that this should continue to be the case. We may suspect that something of the rationalism and humanism of the sixteen-forties and fifties must have survived to help the common people to resist the economic and ideological pressures to which the defeat of the Revolution had laid them open; but from the nature of the case, evidence is hard to come by.[5]

In wider sociological terms we can see changes which mark a transition to the modern world. In place of a single state church based on compulsory geographical communities of families—parishes—we get religious toleration—membership of congregations by individuals who chose them. Roger Williams spoke of membership of a church as though it were no different from membership of a City trading company. In towns, sects offered substitute communities for those which immigrants had lost.[6] In place of the communal ceremonial and ritual of the Middle Ages, preaching became all-important. Mediaeval churches were built as places in which the host was elevated and processions were held; the dissenting chapel, and Wren's churches, were auditoria for the pulpit. It was a shift from a civilization of the eye—images are the books of the

5. *The World Turned Upside Down*, chaps. 8 and 17. Cf. pp. 49–50 and 71–72 above and 87 below.

6. Thomas, *Religion and the Decline of Magic*, p. 153.

illiterate—to a civilization of the ear. The parish slowly changes from being a community centre to a taxing body, part of the government machinery, concerned with relief, not amenities. The latter were looked after by other, voluntary, organizations. The idea of the parish as a democratic community survived in radical thought from the Levellers and Winstanley to Thomas Spence. But oligarchy triumphed in 1660, and was unshaken in 1688. Although England was for the upper and middle classes freer than any country in Europe (except perhaps the Netherlands), the survival of monarchy, House of Lords, and bishops was a powerful preservant of snobbism and deference.

At the same time that social radicalism was challenging traditional certainties, trade was widening intellectual horizons. Hobbes compared the American Indians to the Anglo-Saxon inhabitants of his country: a new historical relativism. India and China offered examples of non-Christian civilizations. The Puritan John Preston had argued, in favour of a natural religion, that the nations lately discovered by the Spaniards have it written on their hearts that there is a God; in the Whitehall Debates of 1648 the Leveller John Wildman made very sophisticated use of the concept of a natural religion. The young Bunyan asked himself whether the Koran—published in English translation in 1649—had not as good traditional authority in Moslem countries as the Bible in Christendom. Such lines of thought were difficult to check. Calvin had said that the Bible was written to the intellectual capacity of its readers, and John Wilkins used this argument in defence of the Copernican astronomy, to explain away Joshua's telling the sun to stand still. Diggers, Ranters, and early Quakers allegorized the Bible stories almost out of historical existence. Milton and Henry Parker thought there could be nothing in the Bible contrary of the good of man, including his temporal good: awkward texts were to be explained in the light of this general principle. Clement Writer and the Quaker Samuel Fisher used the contradictions and inconsistencies of the Bible to argue that it could not be the Word of God. John Webster suggested that it had been mistranslated in order to maintain belief in witchcraft. Again such thoughts could lead far. Biblical criticism was paralleled by an abandonment of arguments from precedent and custom in favour of arguments from reason and utility. It was another aspect of the great revolution in human thought which we have been considering. It is difficult for us to think ourselves back into the mental processes of a pre-rational, pre-utilitarian, authoritarian, precedent-dominated society.

This revolution in human thought echoed from England all over Europe (including Scotland) and North America. In Charles I's reign the English ruling class still aped Italian, Spanish, and French fashions and ideas; after 1688 Harrington, Locke, Newton, Hume, and Adam Smith gave the lead to the whole of Europe. Richardson and Fielding, building on seventeenth-century spiritual autobiographies, and on the writings of Bunyan and Defoe, created the novel, the dominant literary form of the modern age.

XII

BUT THE IMMEDIATE post-revolutionary hostility towards "enthusiasm" had damaging effects on literature. "Inspiration," Davenant thought, was "a dangerous word," in literature no less than in religion.[1] The imagination of the writer must be subordinated to the rules approved by the society. Dr. P. W. Thomas has traced the rise of Augustan classicism to the defeated royalists in the early fifties, and has suggested that it was the product of élitist intellectuals faced by a hostile and too powerful plebs. In the reign of Augustus Rome's new men had been defeated in a bitter political struggle, and an aristocracy had reentrenched itself in power. The new classicism in England was expressed by the balanced rhymed couplet, from which the revolutionary Milton had hoped to liberate verse.[2]

From about the middle of the seventeenth century rational men ceased to claim to have seen a vision or heard the voice of God. In 1660–62 a series of seditious pamphlets cited prodigies and prognostications as arguments against the legitimacy of the restored Stuart régime. Ironically, some of what seemed the most absurd claims to have seen visions in the sky have been accepted by modern scholars as evidence of interesting meteorological phenomena.[3] The *Annus Mirabilis* of John Dry-

1. Davenant, *Gondibert*, p. 22.
2. P. W. Thomas, *Sir John Berkenhead, 1617–1679: A Royalist Career in Politics and Polemics* (Oxford: Clarendon Press, 1969), chaps. 5–7.
3. D. J. Schove, "English Aurorae of A.D. 1660/61," *Journal of the British Astronomical Association* 62: 38–41, 62–65; "London Aurorae of A.D. 1661," ibid., 63; 266–70, 321–25. See my *The World Turned Upside Down*, p. 235.

den, F.R.S., did not deny that signs and portents could teach historical lessons, but argued that the authors of the pamphlets had drawn the wrong conclusions.[4] But gradually public opinion, again faced with competing explanations, came to reject arguments from portents and providences altogether. Put crudely, if Oliver Cromwell had not accepted the doctrine of providences, he would have been much less likely to join the Army in revolt in May 1647, and to force the execution of the King in January 1649. Herein lay the revolutionary significance of the doctrine, and the importance of Sprat's opposition to it. It is part of the contribution which the Royal Society made to the reconsolidation of society.

The religious-rationalist utopian hopes for a better world were defeated. Puritanism turned slowly into sectarian nonconformity, the sects withdrew from politics. Parsons and J.P.s resumed control over the moral behaviour of the poor. Monarchy was restored to preside over the rule of gentlemen and merchant oligarchies, the Royal Society was established to check the advance of mechanic atheism. The mechanical philosophy replaced the universe of correspondences and analogies, poetic because integrated, animistic, magical. In its place rose the abstract, empty, unfriendly mathematical universe of the Newtonians. From the late seventeenth century it became normal for poets to feel themselves alienated from their society, sometimes to the point of madness. One thinks of Rochester, Otway, Lee, Swift, Gray, Collins, Smart, Chatterton, Blake, Cowper, Clare. There was an emotional vacuum.

Milton's was the last great epic, the last major attempt at a totally integrated world view. It was followed by the half-century of the mock epic, a confession of defeat. Better poets like Dryden and Pope translated the great traditional epics: this was defeat too. Only after the mid-eighteenth century does the

4. McKeon, *Politics and Poetry in Restoration England*, part II *passim*.

novel fill the vacuum left by the epic and the drama of conflict, silenced not by Jeremy Collier's attack on the stage but by the ending of the fruitful social tensions which had prevailed for the century before he wrote. Drama of any quality written in English is henceforth almost exclusively the work of Irishmen —Congreve, Goldsmith, Sheridan, Wilde, Shaw, Yeats, Synge, O'Casey, Becket. The novel can be seen as the bourgeois equivalent of the epic, but realistically earthbound as the epic could not be. The novel's conflicts are internal, those of developing character, rather than external, those of military achievement. Seen in this perspective Milton's *Paradise Regained* looks forward to the novel rather than back to the epic. The epic of the poor, *Pilgrim's Progress,* depicts a man with a burden on his back, which cannot be shaken off in this life. But it too is about how we should live on earth.

Morally the worst period of all for England in transition seems to have been the opening decades of the eighteenth century. They were years of returning political stability, of great economic progress of the brutal kind depicted in E. P. Thompson's *Whigs and Hunters.* They also saw the establishment of England's monopoly of the slave trade, the scandal of the South Sea Bubble, and the piling up of death sentences for offences against property. They produced Mandeville's *Fable of the Bees,* which stood traditional morality on its head by arguing that private vices were public benefits, as well as *Gulliver's Travels,* whose hero ultimately came to prefer horses to the nearly human Yahoos. I quoted Swift's *Modest Proposal* suggesting that the natives of England's first colony would benefit themselves if they served up their children as food for their English rulers. Gay's *The Beggars' Opera* and Fielding's *Jonathan Wild* both likened government to a gang of thieves—Winstanley's image three generations earlier. Even Robinson Crusoe found life tolerable only outside civilization, thus side-stepping the issue. A century earlier the Pilgrim Fathers had crossed the ocean, in the hope of coming back to a reformed England; but the ex-nonconformist, ex-Monmouthite Defoe saw no such hope. He sold his pen to the highest bidder. The literary high priest during this period was Addison, who saw it as his function to teach piety and the bourgeois virtues to backwoods gentlemen, to refine nonconformist shopkeepers and their wives, to demonstrate that *Paradise Lost* was an orthodox poem. The ethos of London was extended to the provinces, to Wales, Scotland, and Ireland, in the common-sense polite prose which the Royal Society had advocated.

A French historian once invited me to write about the English Revolution and the rights of man. I started by assuming that proclamations of natural rights were things that happened in America, France, or Russia, and that plain blunt Englishmen did not indulge in such fancies. But as usual, a little attention to historical fact exploded generalizations about national character. It is true that the English Revolution produced no grandiose legislative pronouncements concerning human rights. But one does not have to look very far before finding sectaries pleading "for natural rights and liberties, such as men have from Adam by birth" (the words are those of the shocked heresy-hunter, Thomas Edwards)[5]; Levellers first claimed the historical rights of Englishmen, then asserted the natural rights of men to liberty, equality, property, self-government, the vote. Others proclaimed a right to engage in industry and trade. The Diggers argued, on natural rights grounds, that "there cannot be a universal liberty till . . . community [of property] be established." But all these were declarations from opposition groups: there were no ringing governmental pronouncements in 1649 or 1688.

When one reflects on later proclamations of a right to liberty which did not apply to slaves, or of rights of man which were

5. T. Edwards, *Gangraena* (London, 1646), part III, p. 9.

enforced by foreign conquest, an Englishman is inclined to draw a little melancholy satisfaction from our reticence on this subject. Yet wrongly. A right once proclaimed, however hypocritically, is there, and can be appealed to later. The one exception from the English Revolution makes the point. It occurs in the manifesto of 1655, in which Cromwell justified his war against Spain as being to avenge Spanish cruelty against the American Indians, since "all great and extraordinary wrongs done to particular persons ought to be considered as in a manner done to all the rest of the human race." The principle comes oddly from a government which still had the blood of countless Irishmen reeking on its hands. But John Milton, who probably drafted the manifesto, no doubt believed what he said; and it is a point which it would still be nice to have taken seriously in international relations. But the general conclusion *is* melancholy. Among the most important intellectual consequences of the English Revolution were its hypocrisies and its lost causes, causes which either survived as underground traditions, or had to be rediscovered by historians. In this, alas, the English Revolution has much in common with other revolutions.

The Reverend Moses Wall, who regarded himself as rather to the left of Milton, gave economic reasons for the failure of the radical revolution in England, which compare interestingly with those of Sir Peter Pett quoted on p. 58 above. "Let us pity human frailty. . . . While people are not free but straitened in accommodations for life, their spirits will be dejected and servile." Before the movement could revive, "there should be an improving of our native commodities, as our manufactures, our fishery, our fens, forests and commons, and our trade at sea, etc., which would give the body of the nation a comfortable subsistence." Then we might hope for "progressency of the nation . . . in liberty and spiritual truths."

A century of economic advance did in fact create a material

basis for democracy. A new spirit was abroad in the second half of the eighteenth century. It came by going back (not always consciously) to the sixteen-forties. Wesley revived something of the popular enthusiasm of the radical sects, though canalizing the irrational protest of the lower orders (for the time being) into safe Tory channels. Wilkes and the Corresponding Society picked up the democratic politics of Levellers and other republicans. Blake and the Romantics went back to Milton and inspiration. The Scottish school took up again some of the sociological insights of Winstanley and Harrington, just as Adam Smith picked up where Petty left off in political economy, and Priestley continued where Boyle had stopped in chemistry. The American Revolution and post-revolutionary American politics strike the historian of seventeenth-century England as rather like a story he has read before.

With the eighteenth-century enlightenment we are in the world of secular bourgeois thought. Its predecessor, the optimistic, secularized belief in progress, of which the Royal Society and Locke were the spokesmen, came only after social stability had been ensured in the later seventeenth century by suppression of the radical revolution. Moses Wall's postulates for a better society (unlike those of Sir Peter Pett) included the abolition of tithes and security of tenure for small proprietors. The economic progress which actually occurred followed Pett's model rather than Wall's. Revolutionary millenarianism had perhaps been the ideology of small craftsmen and yeomen whose fate it was to be squeezed out by the advance of capitalism in England over the next two centuries.[6] When the time for organized democratic political action came, it took new forms. Millenarianism played a small part in "the making of the English working class," but only a small part.

6. See Barry Barnes, *Interests and the Growth of Knowledge* (London: Routledge & Kegan Paul, 1977), p. 80.

Finally, a point that is not normally made in relation to the "Puritan" Revolution. One of its legacies was a conviction of the goodness of matter and the body, of the desirability of the pursuit of happiness on earth. Winstanley and the Diggers called for "Glory here," on earth now, not in heaven at a date subsequently to be announced. *Paradise Lost, Paradise Regained*, and *Samson Agonistes* are about how to live on earth. Milton does not offer the consolations of the after-life, as Bunyan did. He does not revel in the sufferings of the crucified Saviour, as Crashawe did; nor gloat over the eternal torments of the damned, as Dante had done and as Cowley did. Milton does not hate the human body, as some Puritans did. He emphasized that Adam and Eve made love *before* the Fall, "whatever hypocrites austerely talk." Adam freely chose to fall with Eve rather than live a life of barren virtue alone "in these wild woods forlorn"—his description of the earthly Paradise without Eve. Milton himself rebuked Adam as "fondly overcome by female charm" in this decision; but the poetry shows that one half of him at least applauded Adam's decision.

Milton wanted freer sexual relationships, divorce for incompatibility of temperament. "Casual adultery" he thought "but a transient injury," "soon repented, soon amended," which can be forgiven "once and again." More important than physical monogamy was the marriage of true minds. The world was not for Milton a vale of tears. He would have agreed with the Founding Fathers of the American republic in adding "the pursuit of happiness" to life and liberty as natural and proper aims of man on earth, and of woman too.

This is one aspect of the legacy of the radical revolution which Milton illustrates: another is the resilience, toughness in defeat, stubborn adherence to what one believes to be right, which was taken over from Puritanism in the best of the nonconformist tradition. Bunyan's Christian almost gave up when he and Hopeful were imprisoned by Giant Despair. But Hopeful said, "Who knows, but that God that made the world may cause that Giant Despair may die?" The Lord Mayor of Mansoul in *The Holy War* agreed: "therefore we dare not despair, but will look for, wait for and hope for deliverance still." In the *De Doctrina Christiana* Milton confronted the utter defeat which had overtaken the cause he believed to be God's. "The man who believes will not be in too much of a hurry (Isaiah 28.16)," he wrote; "he puts his mouth in the dust, and says, 'Perhaps there is hope' (Lamentations 3.29)." Adam and Eve shed "some natural tears" when they were expelled from Paradise; but Adam's pre-view of the horrors of human history did not stop them setting out to face the future with humble courage. *Paradise Regained* shows the Son of God—"all men are Sons of God"—resisting the temptation to premature political action, preparing for his nobler task of converting mankind. In *Samson Agonistes* the defeated, blinded leader, who has led his people astray, learns from suffering, squalor and degradation to prepare for the moment when God will deliver the Philistines into his hands—or rather, not the Philistines, but their aristocracy and priests, the especial enemies of the radicals in the post-restoration years. Change was still possible. There was still hope for the people of England with whom Milton had become so impatient after 1649. The return of bishops in 1660 no doubt reminded him that in 1641 he had blamed popular ignorance on to those whose policy had "with a most inhuman cruelty . . . put out the people's eyes." So now, when Samson pulled down the temple of Dagon, Milton tells us—with no biblical authority whatsoever—that "the vulgar only 'scaped who stood without."

Dagon's temple survived longer than Milton and his peers expected or would have wished; but it is no accident that radicals like Blake, the early Wordsworth, and Shelley looked back to Milton for poetic inspiration, no less than the Wilkesites and the Chartists looked back to the radicals of the English

Revolution for political inspiration in their struggle against the inheritors of the consensus of 1688.

Acknowledgments

I should like to express my gratitude to the University of Wisconsin, which honoured me by inviting me to deliver these lectures; and to all those who helped to make my visit to Madison so enjoyable, especially Morton Rothstein and Edward Gargan.

Index

Bristol, 37
British empire, 4, 42, 90
Broghill, Roger Boyle, Lord; later Earl of
  Orrery, 61
Browne, Sir Thomas, 50, 77
Buckingham, George Villiers, Duke of,
  18, 51
Bull, John, 25
Bunting, Jabez, 78
Bunyan, John, 13–14, 47, 50, 53, 66,
  78, 80, 81, 88
Burnet, Gilbert, Bishop of Salisbury,
  19
Burrough, Edward, 58

Calvin, John, 80
Calvinism, 60, 64, 70, 71, 72, 79
Calvinists: Dutch, 72; French, 72
Cambridge, 46, 54, 55
Capital, accumulation of, 37, 41
Capitalism, 39, 43, 66, 87
Cavaliers, 12, 17
Censorship, 7, 14, 44, 46–47, 48–49; ec-
  clesiastical, 14, 54; Chekhov and, 47;
  self-, 51
Charles I, King of England, 3, 7, 11, 12,
  13, 14, 16, 18, 19, 27, 28, 29, 59, 69,
  72, 81, 83
Charles II, King of England, 10, 11, 12,
  14, 15, 19, 20, 23, 24, 25, 27, 28, 30,
  41, 45, 46, 58, 59, 61, 63, 68, 69, 73
Chartists, the, 89
Chatterton, Thomas, 83
Chekhov, Anton, 47
Chemistry, 87
Child, Sir Josiah, 43
Children, death rate of poor, 51
China, 4, 80
Church of England, the, 3, 7, 13, 24, 53–
  57, 62, 68–70, 73–79
Churchwardens, 56, 76
Civil service, 26, 41
Civil war of 1642–46, 7, 18, 44, 50, 57
Clare, John, 83
Clarendon, Edward Hyde, Earl of, Lord
  Chancellor, 11, 12, 13, 44
Clarendon Code, 14, 24
Clarkson, Lawrence, 77, 78
Class, 40; analyses, 44
—structure: two-class, 39, 52, 55; influ-
  ence of, 43
Classicism, Augustan, 82

Clergy, Anglican, 13, 14, 18, 24, 49,
  54–57, 71, 83
Clothing depression (1620s), 17
Coke, Sir Edward, 5, 48
Colbert, Jean Baptiste, 42
College of Physicians, 51
Collier, Jeremy, 53, 84
Collins, William, 83
Colour bar, 38
Comenian reformers, 65
"Commercial Revolution," 36, 37, 90
Common law, 5, 20, 29, 40, 52, 57,
  65
"Common man," 27–28, 32
Common people, 12, 65, 78
Commons, House of, 12, 13, 18, 29,
  30, 57, 69
Commonwealth, 11, 12, 19, 22, 26,
  36, 41, 59
Communism, 7, 65
Congregationalists, 73, 74
Congreve, William, 84
Conscription, 24
Constitution, the English, 4, 27, 31
Consumer goods, 36
Contractualism, 60
Conventicles, 56
Convocation of Canterbury, 57
Coppe, Abiezer, 78
Coppin, Richard, 78
Copyholders, 35, 87
Corbet, John, 11, 68–69
Correspondences (theory), 66, 83
Corresponding Society, 87
Corruption, political, 30
Cotton, Sir Robert, 18
Couplets, rhymed, 61, 82
Coverley, Sir Roger de, 32
Cowley, Abraham, 88
Cowper, William, 83
Craftsmen, 9, 87
Crashawe, Richard, 88
Cromwell, Oliver, Lord Protector: and
  land tax, 17; and the military, 19, 23,
  25, 26, 32, 36; compared to Stalin and
  Mao-tse-tung, 23; and union of 1652,
  42; foreign policy of, 59; and state
  church, 73; mentioned, 10, 12, 15, 16,
  19, 53, 56, 60, 61, 62, 66, 68, 72, 83,
  86
Culpeper, Nicholas, 49
Customs revenue, 36

Dante Alighieri, 88
Davenant, Charles, 43
Davenant, Sir William, 25, 82
Davies, Godfrey, 10
Davis, R., 36
Death: penalty, 40; rate, 51; sentence, 84
Debt, law of, 29
Declaration of Indulgence (1672), 73–74
Defoe, Daniel, 50, 72, 81, 84, 85
Deism, 61, 66, 72, 77, 78
Democracy, 4, 9, 12, 27, 35, 67, 79, 86–87
Demography, 43
Denne, Henry, 78
D'Ewes, Sir Simonds, 49
Diaries, 50
Diggers, the, 30, 32, 44, 50, 59, 80, 85, 88
Discipline, ecclesiastical, 13, 69, 71
Discourse for a King and Parliament, A (1660), 11
Dissenters, 20, 24–25, 31–32, 54, 55–56, 69, 74, 77, 83, 85, 88
Dissenting academies, 55
Divine right, 28, 66
Divorce, 49, 88
Donne, John, 76
Dover, 68
Dryden, John, 25, 58, 59, 60, 68, 82–83, 84
Duelling, 25
Dury, John, 21, 73
Dutch wars, 23, 36, 59

"Economic man," 43
Economics: motivated conquest of Ireland, 23; affects of English Revolution on English, 34–43; and politics, 43; science of, 43, 65; free discussion of, 54; assumptions about role of, 58–59; post-Restoration, 59, 87; Latitudinarian attitude toward capitalistic, 63
Education: public schools, 31; of the poor, 50; ecclesiastical control of, 54; divisions within and failings of, 55–56; ideal of free, 67
Edwards, Thomas, 85
Edward the Confessor, 53
Eikon Basilike, 27
Elizabeth I, Queen of England, 74
Emigration, 8, 16
Enclosure, 18, 38, 39, 40, 43
Enlightenment, the, 5, 87

"Enthusiasm," 60, 61, 62, 64, 66, 77, 82, 87
Epics, 83, 84
Episcopacy, 7, 13, 14, 53
Europe, 16, 25, 26, 31, 36, 38, 42, 72, 80, 81
Eve, 78, 88, 89
Excise, 41
Excommunication, 56, 75

Fall of man, the, 45, 59, 78, 88
Family, the, 7, 39
Fenstanton Baptists, 75
Feudal tenures, 34
Fielding, Henry, 40, 81, 84
Fifth Monarchists, 71
Filmer, Sir Robert, 60
Fisher, Samuel, 81
Foreign policy, 3, 14–15, 26, 27, 31, 59
Fox, George, 8, 16, 54, 78
Foxe, John, 57
France, 4, 23, 24, 26, 31, 41, 42, 72, 81, 85
Franchise, 3, 7, 12, 29, 31, 40, 85
Freeholders, 9, 35
French Revolution, 9, 23–24, 31, 41–42
Fuller, Thomas, 10

Game laws, 30
Gay, John, 84
General practitioners, 51
Gentry, 3, 8, 9, 11, 14, 18, 20, 24, 26, 27, 31, 40, 41, 52, 54–57, 83
Germany, 4, 31
Ghana, 38
Gibbon, Edward, 28, 38
Gilbert, William, 49
Glanvill, Joseph, 77
Glorious Revolution (1688), 41
Goldsmith, Oliver, 51, 84
Goodman, Godfrey, Bishop of Gloucester, 48
Goodwin, John, 71
Gordon Riots, the, 31
Gosson, Stephen, 53
Government: parliamentary, 4; representative, 4; popular, 12; local, 20, 54, 74; central, 54; self-, 85
Grammar schools, 50
Graunt, John, 43
Gray, Thomas, 83
Greville, Fulke, Lord Brooke, 48

Lords, House of, 3, 7, 10, 12, 14, 16, 26, 29, 30, 80
Louis XIV, King of France, 23, 41, 72
Lower class: new freedoms for, 7, 67; led away from radicalism, 8; as ripe for revolt, 17–18; and fighting Antichrist, 18, 57; excluded from militia, 20; effect of inclusion of, into politics, 29; and game laws, 30; and the constitution, 31; Toryism, 31–32; nostalgia of, for Merrie England, 32; rights of, 40; new taxes on, 41; and education, 55; morality of, 70, 83; and Presbyterianism, 71; church attendance by, 76; mentioned, 14, 19, 52, 79, 82, 87
Ludlow, Edmund, 44

Machine-breaking, 40
Magic, 27–28, 64–65, 66, 83
Major-Generals, the, 32
Manchester, Edward Montagu, Earl of, 28
Mandeville, Bernard de, 43, 84
Mao-tse-tung, 23
Market: imperial, 26, 36, 37; home, 38; production for, 41; centralization of, 42; economy, 43; expansion of, 43; and medical practice, 51; society and nature, 63; emergence of new professions in, 65; mentioned, 79
Marseilles, 42
Marvell, Andrew, 25, 45
Marx, Karl, 14, 43
Mason, John, 58
Mathematics, 64
Mazarin, Cardinal, 26
Mechanical philosophy, 63, 64, 65, 66, 83
Mede, Joseph, 48, 57
Medicine, 51, 52, 65, 66
M.P.'s, 55
Merchants, 3, 8, 9, 36, 37, 51, 83
Methodism, 79
Middle Ages, 79
Middle class: austerity of 19th-century, 30; 19th-century enfranchisement of, 31; wives, economic role of, 39; leisured, 51; professional, 55; freedom of, 80; mentioned, 79
Military values, 25, 30
Militia, 11, 16, 20, 30, 42
Millar, Oliver, 51
Millenarianism, 5, 57–58, 59, 60, 87

Milton, John, 5, 7, 27, 30, 45, 46, 47–48, 49, 50, 53, 62, 66, 67, 68, 70, 71, 77, 78, 80, 82, 83, 84, 85, 86, 87, 89
Mobility, 7, 31, 35, 56
Mobs: anti-Catholic, 18; London, 18; church and King, 31; manipulated, 31; the Mob, 35
Monarchy: restoration of, 3, 83; inadequacy of foreign policy of, 15, 26; abolition of, 16; social advantages of, 27; appeal of, to ordinary people, 27–28; manipulated, 28, 31; absolute, 29; protection of business by restored, 30; legend of, 53; obedience to, and doctrine of original sin, 60; mentioned, 12, 14, 29, 80
Monck, George. *See* Albemarle, Duke of
Monied interest, the, 41
Monmouth, James Scott, Duke of, 13, 16
Monmouth's rebellion, 19
Monogamy, 88
Monopolies, 41, 42
Morality: of lower class, 25, 69, 70, 83; and theology, 72; of Presbyterian discipline, 75; and secularization of thought, 78; at start of 18th century, 84–85; mentioned, 25
Moral law, 71
Mordaunt, John, Lord, 11
More, Henry, 77
Mornet, Daniel, 5
Mortalism, 5, 61, 77
Moyle, Henry, 27
Muggleton, Lodowick, 70, 77
Muggletonians, the, 73, 77, 78
Mun, Thomas, 42–43

Napier, John, Lord, 57
"Natural rulers," 3, 8, 9, 16, 17, 19, 20, 30, 32
Naunton, Sir Robert, 48
Navigation Acts, the, 36, 58
Navy, the, 20, 25, 36, 41, 42, 59
Nayler, James, 78
Nedham, Marchamont, 21, 50
Negroes, African, 24, 38
Netherlands, the, 4, 23, 43, 48, 49, 80
Neville, Henry, 27
Newcastle, 15
Newcastle, Margaret, Duchess of, 44
Newcome, Henry, 74
New England, 16, 37

New Model Army, 16, 17, 19, 49, 75
Newspapers, 46, 49
Newton, Sir Isaac, 3, 5, 57, 58, 63, 64, 66, 77, 81, 83
Newtonians, the, 66
Noble savage, the, 38
Nonconformists. *See* Dissenters
Non-resistance, doctrine of, 13
North, Sir Dudley, 43
Notestein, Wallace, 76
Novel, the, 39, 51, 81, 84
Noy, William, 18

O'Casey, Sean, 84
Organization, freedom of, 7, 9, 54
Oroonoko (Behn), 38
Othello, 38
Otway, Thomas, 83
Overton, Richard, 77
Owen, John, 58, 74
Oxford, 46, 53, 54, 55

Pacifism, 16, 54, 60
Pamphlets, 49, 50–51, 83
Papists, 49. *See also* Roman Catholicism
Parker, Henry, 80
Parliament, 3, 4–5, 12, 16, 18, 19, 25, 26, 29, 39, 45, 65, 69, 90; Rump of the Long, 12, 19, 23; Long, 12, 24, 41; Protectorate Parliaments, 24; Cavalier, 24
Parliamentarians, the, 12
Parishes, 79, 80
Pascal, Blaise, 66
Paupers, 9, 35
Peasantry, the, 42, 66
Peers. *See* Aristocracy
Pembroke, William Herbert, 3rd Earl of, 18
Pentateuch, the, 72
Pepys, Samuel, 11, 25, 50
Perfectibility of man, 49
Perkins, William, 62
Persecution, religious, 54
Pett, Sir Peter, 58, 86, 87
Petty, Sir William, 43, 87
Philosophy, licensing of books on, 46
Pocahontas, 38
Poets, 48, 51, 83
"Political arithmetic," 43
Political theory: and Walter Ralegh, 5; dominated by questions of power, 17;

Hobbesian, 20; shift in, from past to future, 60
Politics: abandonment of, by sects, 14, 24, 54, 74, 83; Quaker withdrawal from, 16, 54; suspicion of ideological, 21; rational discussion of, 27; effect of incursion of poor into, 29; wage labourers' lack of independence in, 35; and economics, 43; licensing of books on, 46; radical, and freedom of press, 49; and pamphleteers, 50; free discussion of, 54; and Second Coming, 58; rejection of "enthusiasm" in, 64, 65; as specialized science, 65; Hobbesian, 66; American post-revolutionary, 87; Leveller democratic, 87
Polygamy, 47, 49
Poor, the: relief for, 32, 75, 80; affects of agricultural boom on, 35; accepted as permanent, 40; mentioned, 13–14. *See also* Lower class
Pope, Alexander, 83
Popery, 62, 72. *See also* Roman Catholicism
Popish Plot, 31
Population, 4, 9, 30, 35, 40
Power: dominates political thought, 17; Hobbesian emphasis on, 20; as justification of authority, 21; and property, 44–45
Preaching, 7, 68, 78, 79
Prerogative, 65
Prerogative courts, 29, 56
Presbyterianism, 11, 66, 70, 71, 73, 75
Press, freedom of the, 7, 9, 46–47, 48, 49. *See also* Censorship
Press-ganging, 24
Preston, John, 62, 80
Priestley, Joseph, 87
Primogeniture, 41
Printing, 46, 49
Private Conference between a Rich Alderman and a Poor Country Vicar, A, 54
Professional class, 51, 79
Professionalism, in the arts, 65
Progress: theory of, 59–60, 87; social, 67; economic, 84, 87
Propaganda, 49, 50, 63
Propertied class: fear of radicalism by, 16; hatred of standing armies, 19, 20; belief of, in King's Evil, 28; legal reform affecting, 29; attitude of, towards pov-

erty, 40; and episcopal church, 56; and concept of the elect, 71; mentioned, 10, 11, 12, 65

Property: private, 7, 78; guaranteed by law, 29, 40; affect of Revolution on security of, 34–35; and liberty, 40; and power, 44–45; sanctity of, 70; and morality, 71; death sentence for crimes against, 84; natural right to, 85; mentioned, 12, 17, 21, 26, 67

Prose styles, 50–51, 85

Protectorate, the, 26, 59, 61

Protestantism, 8, 13, 17–18, 23–24, 39, 73

Providence, 4, 44, 45, 63, 83

Prynne, William, 11, 53

Public schools, 31

Purgatory, 77

Puritanism, 34, 39, 53, 62, 64, 68, 69–70, 73, 83, 88–89

Puritans, 32, 37, 53, 62, 71

Putney Debates, 12

Pyrenees, Peace of, 23

Quakers, the, 16, 50, 53, 54, 59, 60, 71, 73, 75, 78, 80

Radicals: opposition to, 3, 29, 66, 89; effects of defeat of, 4, 8–9, 16, 35, 38, 54, 86; influence of, surviving the Restoration, 10–15, 16, 90; threat of, to New Model Army, 16; and taxes by consent, 27; English, vs. French, Russian, and Chinese, 32; demanded security of tenure for copyholders, 35; and censorship, 46–47, 49; attack on specialization of professions by, 52; utopian, 59; Latitudinarians denounced, 62; and Royal Society, 64; growth of, 64; theological, and concept of hell, 70; and Cromwell's state church, 73; and sin, 79; see parish as democratic community, 80; social, 80; and "enthusiasm," 87; view of sexual relationships, 88; and the nonconformist tradition, 88–89; mentioned, 7, 20, 24, 71, 81

Raleigh, Sir Walter, 5

Ranters, the, 50, 71, 78, 80

Rationalism, 78, 79, 82–83

Reason, 66–67, 81

Reform: social, 7; legal, 7, 29, 55; political, 55; lack of educational, 55, 67

Religion, 12, 59; natural, 63, 80; rejection of "enthusiasm" in, 64, 82; new rational, 66; affects of Revolution on, 68–74

Republic, 3, 7, 11, 14–15, 19, 26, 27, 30

Republicanism, 15, 19, 20

"Republicans, classical," 47

Reresby, Sir John, 10–11

Restoration, of 1660: attitudes toward, 10–15; mentioned, 5, 8, 25, 30, 34, 36, 40, 45, 55, 58, 60, 68, 76

Restoration comedy, 50

Rhineland, 23

Richardson, Samuel, 81

Richmondshire, 76

Rights: of juries, 40; of labourers, 40; ancient, 45; human, 85; natural, 85; of man, 85; to happiness, 88

Riots: anti-enclosure, 18; of 1688–89, 19; Gordon, 31; Sacheverell, 31

Ripon, Treaty of, 18

Roberts, R. S., 51

Robinson, Matthew, 76

Rochester, John Wilmot, Earl of, 83

Roman Catholicism, 20, 24, 71, 72, 73

Romantics, the, 87

Rome, 16, 82

Rous, Francis, 21

Royalists, 22, 25, 50, 82

Royal Society of London, 50, 55, 59, 60, 61, 62, 63–64, 77, 83, 85, 87

Ruling class, the, 7, 8, 10, 17, 28, 33, 78, 81

Russia, 85

Russian revolution, 9, 23–24, 41–42

Rymer, Thomas, 38

Sabbatarianism, 68, 75

Sabbath Act (1677), 69

Sacheverell, Henry, 74

Sacheverell riots, 31

St. Paul, 21

Samson, 89

Scarcity: economy of, 43

Schlatter, R. B., 69

Science: and Bacon, 5; licensing of books on, 46; during the Restoration, 63–66 passim; natural, 65; mentioned, 55

Scotland, 13, 18–19, 23, 26, 42, 81, 85

Scottish school of sociologists, 43, 87

Scroggs, Sir William, Lord Chief Justice, 46

Second Coming, the, 58
Sectaries: utopianism of, 59; "enthusiasm" of, 61; and state church, 73; appeal of, to lower class, 76; mentioned, 11, 49, 54, 85
Sects, the: abandonment of politics by, 14, 83; "enthusiasm" of radical, 62, 87; and magic, 64; concept of hell, 70; work ethic of, 71, 75, 76; and state church, 73, 76; community in towns offered by, 79; mentioned, 8, 14, 16, 40, 42, 54
Secularization of thought, 44, 78
Shaftesbury, Anthony Ashley-Cooper, Earl of, 12, 16, 31
Shakespeare, William, 38, 48
Shaw, George Bernard, 84
Shelley, Percy Bysshe, 89
Sheridan, Richard, 84
Shipping, 36
Sibbes, Richard, 62
Sin: poverty as, 40; doctrine of original, 60; vs. crime, 70; idleness as, 75; democracy as, 78–79
Slavery, 36, 38, 40, 85
Slave trade, 24, 26, 36, 37, 84
Smart, Christopher, 83
Smith, Adam, 40, 44, 81, 87
Societies for the Reformation of Manners, 69
Society for the Propagation of the Gospel, 37
Socinianism, 49, 77
South, Robert, 56
South Sea Bubble, the, 84
Soviet Union, 4, 24, 41
Spain, 4, 8, 17, 18, 23, 25, 37, 72, 80, 81, 86
Spanish America, 36, 37
Spanish Succession, War of, 37
Speech, freedom of, 14, 48, 49–50, 54, 64
Spelman, Sir Henry, 49
Spence, Thomas, 80
Sprat, Thomas, Bishop of Rochester, 25, 58, 62, 83
Stalin, Joseph, 23
Standard of living, 35
Steam engine, the, 55
Stubbe, Philip, 53
Swift, Jonathan, 31, 38, 83, 84
Synge, John, 84

Taxation, 16, 19, 27, 36, 41, 57, 58, 80
Taylor, Thomas, 48
Temple, Sir William, 50
Theatre, 53, 84
Thirty Years War, 18, 23, 72
Thomas, P. W., 2
Thomas, K. V., 64–65
Thompson, E. P., 84
Tillotson, John, Archbishop of Canterbury, 69
Tithes, 17, 35, 56, 57, 87
Toland, John, 66
Toleration, religious, 7, 24–25, 54, 56, 73, 79
Toleration Act, of 1689, 24, 77
Tories, 20, 32, 38, 87
Toryism, lower-class, 31–32
Trade: gentry employed in, 26, 41; and kingship, 30–31; capitalist development of, 34; imperial, 36; re-export, 36; restraints on control of, 40, 43; in towns and religious freedom, 56; religious promotion of, 69; widens intellectual horizons, 80; natural right to engage in, 85; mentioned, 58
Trade unions, 40
Trevor-Roper, Hugh, 9

Union of England and Scotland, 1707, 42
Unitarianism, 66, 77
Universities: exclusion of nonconformists from, 54; and training of Anglican clergy, 55
Utilitarianism, 67, 81

Van Dyke, Sir Anthony, 51
Venice, 4
Vietnam, 5
Villages, 24, 31, 32, 35, 57, 66
Virtue: and profit, 69; and conscience, 70
Voluntary Societies, 32

Wage labour, 35, 39, 78
Wales, 42, 85
Wall, Reverend Moses, 86, 87
Waller, Edmund, 25
Wapping, 15
Ward, Seth, Bishop of Salisbury, 55
Water communications, 42
Water Stratford, 58
Webster, Charles, 65
Webster, John, 81

Wentworth, Sir Thomas, Earl of Strafford, 18
Wesley, John, 8, 54, 78, 87
Wesleyanism, 24
West Indies, 16, 24, 36, 37, 38
Whigs, 9, 20, 31, 32, 38
Whinney, Margaret, 51
Whitehall Debates, the (1648), 80
Whitfield, George, 78
Whole Duty of Man, The, 13
Wilde, Oscar, 84
Wildman, John, 80
Wilkes, John, 87
Wilkesites, 89
Wilkins, John, Bishop of Chester, 55, 62, 80
William III, King of England, 19, 20, 23, 26, 28

Williams, Roger, 79
Wilson, Arthur, 48
Winstanley, Gerrard, 14, 27, 32, 35, 43, 65, 67, 77, 78, 80, 84, 87, 88
Witchcraft, 50, 81
Witches, 64, 66, 77
Women, 7, 39, 51
Worcester House Declaration (1660), 69
Worcestershire, 76–77
Wordsworth, William, 89
Work ethic, 39, 75
Wren, Sir Christopher, 79
Writer, Clement, 81

Yeats, William Butler, 84
Yeomen, 87
York, James, Duke of. *See* James II
Yorkshire, 15